THE UNITED STATES AND THE WORLD COURT

BOOKS BY

DENNA FRANK FLEMING

The United States and the World Court

*The Treaty Veto
of the American Senate*

*The United States
and the League of Nations, 1918–20*

*The United States
and World Organization, 1920–33*

While America Slept

Can We Win the Peace?

THE
UNITED STATES
AND THE
WORLD COURT

By

Denna Frank Fleming

Professor of Political Science
Vanderbilt University

DOUBLEDAY, DORAN AND COMPANY, INC.

Garden City, New York

1945

TO

NORMAN H. DAVIS

*Ambassador of Peace for
Four Presidents*

Preface

THIS BOOK is a continuation of the author's studies of the handling of treaties for peace by the United States Senate. It is critical of the Senate's long-established ways of killing peace treaties—of its glacial pace in considering them, of its deadly habit of trying to "perfect" great multilateral treaties for our benefit alone, of its scientific technique for slowly carving the life out of peace machinery by "reservations," of its egotism in assuming obedience to its sovereign will by the governments of sixty other sovereign nations.

Should these descriptions of the Senate's habits seem severe the reader can moderate them, if he feels that this account of our attempts to support the World Court does not bear them out. That story is told here in close relation to the Senate's more catastrophic obstruction of the League of Nations Covenant. That was the tragedy which dominated our handling of the World Court—and our national destiny—in the whole period of the lost peace. What the Senate did to the World Court was the aftermath of the main event. Indeed, the ultimatums so consistently laid down to the members of the World Court could not have been delivered had the Senate not continued to live under the spell of the great obstructive power which it had displayed in 1919–20.

7

In the closing chapters the author has tried to relate the frustrations of the World Court period to the swiftly developing catastrophe in which we are now enveloped, and to the future role of the rule which permits one sixteenth of our Congress to mutilate treaties. After all, it is the future which counts, that future of organized, governed international relations with rising standards of living which is wide open to us—or that future of bigger and better wars in which the marvels of science are prostituted to ever more successful death dealing. We have demonstrated our obstructive and destructive powers, but can we build an enduring civilization? And can we play our part in an ordered world within the limitations of the noose which the Senate's treaty veto constitutes?

I am indebted to Lieutenant Elliott Trimble for vital assistance in research. His able investigation of the same subject in my seminar is responsible for many of the facts in the following pages. A research grant from the Institute of Training and Research in the Social Sciences at Vanderbilt University gave timely aid to the study and my thanks are due also to Manley O. Hudson and Arthur Sweetser for helpful criticism of the first eight chapters. The opinions expressed are, of course, solely my own.

D. F. FLEMING

Nashville
November 11, 1944

Contents

CONTENTS

THE UNITED STATES AND THE WORLD COURT

CHAPTER I

The American Origins of the World Court

THE AMERICAN DEMAND for a world court is more than a century old. It arose from the political success of our union. If thirteen sovereign states could combine in a federal union, successfully admit thirty-five new states and settle their disputes without war, why should other sovereign states continue to fight?

As early as February 1832 the Massachusetts Senate voted that "some method should be established for the amicable and final adjustment of all international disputes."[1] What this method should be was indicated by the role of our own Supreme Court. If the many states of our union could agree that all their differences should be settled by a national Supreme Court, why couldn't the nations do likewise?

Judicial Settlement Successful Between the United States. In the early years of the Republic there was, to be sure, strong hostility among us against our own Supreme Court. For several decades many Americans regarded that Court as "foreign." "We will resist every idea of having our suits declared by foreigners." This sentence was not uttered by a Hearst paper in the 1920s, but by Judge Todd of Kentucky, in 1802, about our own Supreme Court. "This court has no more right to meddle with our questions than has the King's Bench in London!" This was the voice not of the Chicago *Tribune* or the New York *Evening Sun,* saving the

15

Republic from an outlandish World Court in 1925; it was the *United States Telegraph,* writing in 1831 about the Supreme Court of the United States. "We know and feel our strength and we will not have our rights destroyed by an alien court." This defiance was not uttered by the New York *Daily News* or the *Saturday Evening Post* in 1935 against an "alien" World Court; it was hurled at the United States Supreme Court by the Boston *Gazette* in 1801.[2]

For some forty years the ability of our high court to settle a serious dispute between two states went untested. Then in 1832 Rhode Island suddenly claimed a hundred square miles of territory which had been long under the administration of Massachusetts. Five thousand people were involved. Massachusetts was so affronted that she wrapped the long-unused robes of sovereignty about her and denied the jurisdiction of the Court. Daniel Webster argued for her that a dispute involving sovereign rights was beyond the jurisdiction of any court of law. There was no law to cover such cases, the same argument used by Senator Borah against the World Court a century later. First codify international law, said Borah; create the law and then the Court can function. But the United States Supreme Court calmly assumed jurisdiction of the Rhode Island case and disallowed it on the old principle that territorial rights so long established were to be considered legal.

During the intervening century the Supreme Court has decided sixty-five issues between our states involving disputes over territory, and, says the leading historian of the Supreme Court, it has never met any form of controversy between the states which it could not solve by resort to some principle of law or equity. Only two of our forty-eight states have never been a party to one of these suits, which have settled grave social and economic disputes, in addition to disputes over territory involving thousands of square miles, in which large bodies of troops had been used and considerable blood spilled.[3]

The demonstrated success of the Supreme Court in the Rhode Island-Massachusetts case of 1832 was reflected in another resolution passed by both houses of the Massachusetts legislature in 1837 and in popular agitation for the calling of a congress of nations to establish an international tribunal. In 1840 a New Hampshire farmer, William Ladd, wrote a famous essay in which he proposed a court of nations, though one without power to enforce either its use or its decisions. It should, however, offer to mediate any existing war and "any difficulty arising between any two or more nations which would endanger the peace of the world."[4]

The idea of an international tribunal was commended by the legislatures of Massachusetts in 1844 and of Vermont in 1852.[5] Continuing the Massachusetts tradition, Charles Sumner introduced a resolution in the United States Senate, in 1872, proposing a tribunal with such authority as to make it a complete substitute for war. Thereafter attention centered on Secretary of State Blaine's proposed Pan-American conference to consider ways of preventing war between the American nations, first projected for 1882, but not held until 1889.

During the previous year 235 members of the British Parliament united in a communication to our government urging the signing of an arbitration treaty between the two countries. The Senate Committee on Foreign Relations reciprocated with a proposed joint resolution on June 13, 1888, adopted in 1890, asking the President to negotiate for arbitration treaties. After further parliamentary exchanges a treaty of arbitration was signed with Great Britain in 1897, but it was emasculated in the Senate by a swarm of amendments and then the sterile remnant failed by four votes to receive the essential two-thirds majority.[6]

Machinery to Encourage Arbitration Established at The Hague. Blocked in this direction, the State Department seized the occasion of the First Hague Conference, called by the Czar of Russia in 1899 to induce rival nations to reduce a level of armaments which he could not equal, to present a plan for a real world court. The American delegates were instructed by Secretary of State John Hay to propose a court "composed of judges chosen on account of their personal integrity and learning in international law by a majority of the members of the highest court in each of the adhering states." The tribunal was to be permanent, always open to all nations, and the contracting nations were to submit all disputes to it, except those which affected their political independence or territorial integrity.[7]

Few of the other delegates were prepared to go so far. They soon deadlocked on the method of electing the judges, and what resulted from their deliberations was a permanent court in name only. Each state agreed to designate four eminent persons who would hold themselves ready to serve as arbitrators, should they be invited by disputing states. The representatives at The Hague of the states belonging to this "court" were designated to serve as an administrative council, to approve its small budget and provide for a registrar who would always be available. The Permanent Court of Arbitration was accordingly only a panel of possible arbitrators, varying from 75 to 150 names, from which contending states might set up an *ad hoc* arbitration tribunal if they chose. It was not a court in any sense of the word.

Nevertheless, this body made it less feasible for governments to maintain that they could not find suitable arbitrators. A center was established to facilitate arbitration, with trained personnel and considerable prestige behind it, and it has been useful. Some twenty-one arbitrations have been held under its auspices, in which sixteen different states participated: France nine times, Great Britain eight times, the United States on six occasions, and eight other states at least twice.[8]

We Propose a World Court in 1907. This is something. It was a beginning, and if there had been no world wars for a century or two the habit of resorting to the Hague panel might have grown. Unfortunately the Russo-Japanese War of 1904–05 gave us definite warning that this was not to be the case. It also stimulated our government to make another effort in the Second Hague Conference of 1907 to secure a permanent world court. This time Secretary of State Elihu Root instructed his delegates to press for obligatory arbitration, in which they failed, and for a permanent court. "It should be your effort," said Mr. Root, "to bring about in the Second Conference a development of the Hague tribunal into a permanent tribunal composed of judges who are judicial officers and nothing else, who are paid adequate salaries, who have no other occupation, and who will devote their entire time to the trial and decision of international causes by judicial methods and under a sense of judicial responsibility. . . . The court should be made of such dignity, consideration, and rank that the best and ablest jurists will accept appointment to it, and that the whole world will have absolute confidence in its judgments."[9] The Conference did "recommend" the establishment of a court of arbitral justice, which would be permanent to the extent that it was to meet once every year, but nothing came of this proposal.[10]

The advantages of a permanent court over arbitration were and are clear and unmistakable. An arbitration tribunal is difficult to constitute. If the two disputing parties insist on having their own nationals as arbitrators, then everything is likely to hinge on who the umpire or odd man on the tribunal is. Often he has been fair, but sometimes distinctly partisan. In any event he has too much importance. The procedure in an arbitration case, also, is too much akin to diplomacy. The tribunal is selected by diplomatic means, after a dispute has become acute, and works usually under a *compromis*, a diplomatic agreement laying down rules for its guidance. The atmosphere favors compromise, giving both sides something instead of judgment according to principles of law. The verdict may contribute to sound precedents, but the tribunal then dissolves. It does not develop its precedents in the future, from case to case, as a permanent court would. The arbitration tribunal is here today and gone tomorrow. It does not remain to defend and build upon its own reputation, and to develop a consistent body of international law.

Yet nothwithstanding these patent advantages of permanent judicial procedure, the failure of our initiatives in the Hague Conferences forced us back upon arbitration as the only available method of advance. The First Hague Conference, too, gave arbitration a strong stimulus. Within five years thirty-three treaties agreeing to arbitrate future disputes had been signed among the powers. In line with this trend the State Department signed, in 1904, a series of rigidly limited treaties excluding all questions relating to "vital interests," "independence," or "honor." Only "legal" questions were to be arbitrated, after a special agreement, or *compromis*, regulating the whole procedure had been agreed upon in each dispute.

Arbitration Treaties Repeatedly Emasculated in the Senate. The Senate amended the treaties by substituting the word "treaty" for "agreement," thus leaving to its future pleasure the whole question as to whether an arbitration should take place. In each case the Senate would decide after a dispute had become too hot to settle by diplomacy. This, said President Theodore Roosevelt, "made shams of the treaties," and he dropped them. He wished "either to take part in something that means something, or else not have any part in it at all."[11]

Four years later a new Secretary of State, Elihu Root, persuaded Roosevelt to compromise with the Senate. He agreed to send the *compromis* of each arbitration to the Senate for its approval, before it was signed, and by 1910 twenty-two new arbitration treaties had been put into force.

This success led President Taft to believe that the time had come to drop the excluding phrases "vital interests, independence, or honor," under which the arbitration of any important dispute could be refused, and put the presumption in favor of arbitration. He therefore negotiated, in 1911, new treaties with Great Britain and France to cover all disputes which were "susceptible of decision by application of the principles of law and equity." Provision was also made for a commission of inquiry, to elucidate facts, define issues, and in certain cases decide whether a question was "justiciable"—that is, arbitrable.

This, said a majority report of the Senate Committee on Foreign Relations written by Senator Henry Cabot Lodge, was unconstitutional. Only a vote of the Senate could send anything to arbitration. Lodge's close friend ex-President Roosevelt, now at odds with Taft, also greeted the new treaties "as an act of maudlin folly"[12] and Lodge attacked them as war breeders, not peace treaties. Ratification meetings in their favor were held all over Britain, and in the United States an almost unanimous press support was buttressed by resolutions from 200 Chambers of Commerce, but without avail. Mr. Lodge thought of a dozen hypothetical issues which might be raised by other nations against us. The portentous dangers lurking in these innocent-appearing arbitration treaties were held up to the public for six months before they were emasculated, on March 7, 1912, by amendments which led President Taft to drop them.

The Technique of Killing Treaties Perfected by 1911. It was in this struggle that the Senate's technique of defeating peace treaties was fully developed. The method is to think of every unpleasant question which might be raised by other powers against the United States and to hold these possible complications before the public for months, asking incessantly for a few simple words in the treaty to ward off each of the alleged temptations of other nations to put the United States in a hole. And if these supposed dangers are denied, the reply is, "Well, if there is no danger, what harm is there in making it clear in the treaty?" "Reservations" and amendments are finally attached to it by an ordinary majority of the Senate (in the 1911 case, 42 to 40), facilitated by the knowledge of the treaty's friends that it must command a two-thirds majority on the final vote.[18]

After 1908 our government had receded from its effort to create a permanent world court to the attempt to achieve arbitration treaties which would bind us in advance of disputes to arbitrate important controversies when they occurred. This endeavor having been frustrated in the Senate, our effort to promote the pacific settlement of disputes tapered off further into the twenty-two Commission of Inquiry treaties proposed by Secretary of State William J. Bryan and approved by the Senate on August 13, 1914, shortly after the First World War broke out.

The Bryan treaties did not provide for arbitration. They called only for a year's delay, during which a commission of inquiry, with a majority of neutral citizens on it, should investigate and report, but without power to act. After the tumultuous haste with which many nations had just stumbled into war it was difficult to argue that a "cooling-off" period was undesirable.

An American Goal. During the century which ended in 1914 the American people and their executive representatives demonstrated a long and persistent interest in promoting the settlement of international disputes by judicial means. We were not constantly aiming at a real world court, but sometimes we were. At other times the goal was arbitration, but always some form of settlement by men at a table, instead of by force. There can scarcely be any question that the idea of a world court was fathered here, born of the success of the United States Supreme Court. Edward W. Bok, leading Philadelphia publisher, did not exaggerate when he said in 1925: "The World Court is essentially our idea. We proclaimed it for years. We argued for it; we labored for it and finally it was worked out, very largely, by the best American brains. It is of American origin. It came into world consciousness because of American initiative; it is American in its conception and in its reflection of our strong national belief in courts of justice."[14]

CHAPTER II

War Becomes the Arbiter

IT WAS CHARACTERISTIC of the century which ended in 1914 that the best thought of forward-looking Americans went into the promotion of international *judicial* processes. Developing freely behind the silent protection of the British Navy, our leaders thought that a few real courts would keep the world in order. Almost no one ever suggested that strong legislative and executive organs of world government would also be required.

The great advocates of judicial institutions would have balked at that, Theodore Roosevelt excepted. The danger and badness of European "politics" was an axiom of faith with them. The American delegates to the First Hague Conference had risen in that distinguished assembly and read with great solemnity the following proclamation: "Nothing contained in this Convention shall be so construed as to require the United States of America to depart from its traditional policy of not intruding upon, interfering with, or entangling itself in the political questions or policy of internal administration of any foreign State; nor shall anything contained in the said Convention be construed to imply a relinquishment by the United States of America of its traditional attitude toward purely American questions."

These magic words soon came to have, to most American leaders, a religious significance. The delegates to the Second Hague Conference were abjured always to keep them in mind. The mystic phrases were intoned even after the catastrophe of 1914, as if their mere utterance would cause the shade of George Washington to strike heretic Americans dumb. At your peril—any "intruding upon, interfering with, or entangling in" political questions!

"Political questions"—these were not for Americans, even after the storm of the First World War broke upon us with the force of an earthquake. To most of us the war was an incredible event. Not one in a hundred had sensed its approach. The world had seemed safe. Peace was taken for granted and its preservation cost us nothing. Leading intellectuals taught that the businessmen and bankers simply would not tolerate another world war. They would shut off the money for it.

Sudden Anarchy. Then it happened. All of the Great Powers, save only the fledgling United States, were suddenly at war, and many lesser nations. A pistol shot at Sarajevo, a swift rush of events, every government protesting that it was not to blame, and then the deluge—millions of men killed, larger numbers maimed for life; tens of millions of lives starved, stunted, and deranged; wealth worth five hundred billion dollars squandered for destructive purposes. No one could deny that Western civilization had broken down catastrophically.

For a time a strong body of opinion led by Elihu Root continued to maintain that world judicial institutions were a sufficient remedy,[1] but moved by the appalling facts of the war, most of our leaders concluded that political organization would be essential. The Hague "court" of arbitration had been brushed aside like a straw in a tornado. Even a real world court could—and would similarly—be ignored by headstrong governments who either wanted war or were willing to accept it as the alternative to losing either prestige or relative position in a balance-of-power world.

The forthright mind of Theodore Roosevelt had already moved ahead to the enforcement of world peace, in his Nobel Peace Prize Address of May 1910. Under the impact of the Great War he maintained unequivocally that we must not only create a judge but "put police power back of the judge." If this was Utopia it was either "Utopia or Hell."[2] President Woodrow Wilson had arrived at that conclusion in the autumn of 1914, as had William H. Taft, who decided that every warmaker must be told, "You have got to keep the peace or have all the rest of us against you." Here was the simple essence of the problem which stared at all the nations in 1914 and which has never ceased to confront them. Millions of words have been used in making the issue complicated and in denying the validity of the obvious solution, but Taft's sentence of 1914 stated the inexorable truth so simply that a child could see it.

The Peace Must Be Enforced. Most thinking Americans did see it. Led by Taft, a League to Enforce Peace was formed in Independence Hall, Philadelphia, on June 17, 1915. The first plank in its platform was "an international court of justice" to which all "justiciable" questions would be submitted, all others to go to conciliation, the joint forces of the League to be used against any state which rejected these procedures.[3]

The thousand distinguished Americans who co-operated to launch the League to Enforce Peace soon expanded to many thousands. It became the greatest organization of aroused citizens which this country had ever known. Its chapters covered the nation. By November 1, 1919, it had 13,000 volunteer speakers on its lists. At its great congress of May 27, 1916, President Wilson accepted its program and Senator Lodge extolled it. He recalled that a year earlier he had said "it is in the search for Utopia that great discoveries have been made. Not failure but low aim is crime."

Few more pregnant truths have been spoken. What a colossal crime it would have been had men of good will failed to make a mighty effort to find a solution for the international anarchy which seared and scorched the earth in 1916. Of that crime we were not guilty. We saw clearly what had to be done and proposed to do it. The "next step," said Lodge, is to put force behind the peace. "We may not solve it in this way, but if we cannot solve it in that way it can be solved in no other." The keen mind of the scholar senator had penetrated to the heart of the problem, but under his leadership the simple truth he had so clearly stated was later so obscured from the people that a second and more deadly world war swiftly came upon them.

In 1916 obscurantism had not begun its work. Ninety-six per cent of our Chambers of Commerce voted that we take the initiative in forming a league of nations and 64 per cent voted for military sanctions to enforce the verdicts of the proposed court and conciliation council.[4] Then the election of 1916 unexpectedly returned Woodrow Wilson to the presidency, by a hairsbreadth, the first Democrat since Andrew Jackson to succeed himself. Men long used to ruling the nation found themselves still on the outside during the greatest crisis of modern times. In April 1917 the United States itself was forced into the war by the demonstrated purpose of Germany to gain world mastery and by a ruthless use of new weapons of war which reduced the international law of the sea to a collection of lifeless words.

Then for two years President Wilson voiced in a series of great speeches a determination to achieve a league of nations with power to keep order in the world. This objective drew little dissent, except for the speech of Senator Lodge, on February 1, 1917, in which he parted company with the idea of a league to enforce peace, and charged that such an organization would enforce oriental immigration upon us. The senator talked of the stern realities and about a league "which may plunge us into war at any moment at the bidding of other nations." Thus was born the deceptive idea that world wars are not our business which mushroomed later into a great self-destroying national delusion.

"Wilson's" League of Nations Opposed. As the First World War drew to a close the American constitutional calendar called for the congressional election of 1918, in which President Wilson asked for a Democratic Congress to enable him to carry through the peacemaking without the opposition of a hostile Senate. He failed by one vote to achieve control of the Senate for his party. The Senate was organized against him. Its entire machinery was to be used to block "his" League of Nations. Even the sacred rule of seniority was violated to pack the Senate Committee on Foreign Relations with a heavy majority of irreconcilable opponents of the League of Nations. Then, with both the Committee and the Senate in his hands, Mr. Lodge could take his time, using as many months as might be needed to mobilize the hatreds and frustrations of the war into a majority against the "Wilson League."

It was a long, uphill fight, but the opposition had the essentials of victory. In mid-December 1918 Lodge and Theodore Roosevelt planned a campaign to emasculate the League with reservations.[5] Simultaneously Lodge and Knox made speeches warning the Peace Conference not to put any constitution for a league of nations into the treaty of peace. This drive was pressed insistently, since it would be an appalling responsibility to hold up the peace treaty itself for months while the emasculation of the League Covenant went forward, but it failed. President Wilson in Paris got the League Covenant written, and even after slightly more than a third of the Senate, all Republicans, had joined a round-robin demand, on March 4, 1919, that the Peace

Conference put the League aside, Wilson was strong enough, with Taft's support, to keep it in the treaty.

A Slow Campaign to Kill the League Indirectly. Those were grim months for the senatorial "cabal," the term first used by George Harvey, one of its chief organizers. On February 21, 1919, Lodge assured Borah that 85 per cent of the Senate was for the League. To both Borah and Senator James E. Watson, who thought "80 per cent of the people are for it," Lodge patiently explained that "the indirect method of reservation" would finally win.[6]

The emasculation of the Covenant by this method was a staggering undertaking, for "it is as certain as anything in the realm of public opinion can be" that in May 1919 the majority of the American people favored the ratification of the Covenant as it stood. This is the verdict of Ruhl J. Bartlett in his illuminating history of *The League to Enforce Peace*.[7] It would take both time and money to reverse the great popular demand for a league of nations strong enough to defend us from the agonies and wastes of other world wars. Much money would be needed to "educate" the nation away from realizing a need so deeply felt. There was accordingly great relief in the cabal when, late in May 1919, two Pittsburgh multimillionaires, Henry C. Frick and Andrew W. Mellon, supplied a financial reservoir which was "both deep and full. All anxiety respecting sinews of war was dispelled."[8]

By the time the Covenant of the League of Nations was laid before the Senate, on July 10, 1919, it had been questioned in that body from every possible angle, week after week, for six months. This process continued through July and August, while Senator Lodge gravely read the enormous treaty of peace to his empty committee room and then opened a forum for all the many groups who were dissatisfied with one or another of the territorial settlements.

Despairing of making headway against these tactics, the President decided in September to take the League to the country. After traveling eight thousand miles and delivering thirty-seven speeches in twenty days he collapsed and was thereafter unable to attempt a compromise with the group of fourteen to eighteen mild reservationist Republican senators. This group combined with the treaty's supporters to reject in mid-October the fifty direct amendments voted by the Committee, but in the process they pledged themselves to vote for "reservations," as Mr. Lodge had expected them to do. Mild, reasonable men can always be counted on to end up in a middle-ground position, but not so the irreconcilables. They openly voted for the reservations only as a means of killing the treaty.

Reservations Adopted. Fourteen reservations were adopted between November 7 and 19, to match the President's Fourteen Points, though this mocking symmetry was spoiled at the end by the voting of a fifteenth reservation to promote Irish independence. The other reservations swept away all possible impediments to our withdrawal from the League; forbade the President to accept any mandates to govern territory; reserved absolute jurisdiction over all "domestic" questions, including "the suppression of traffic in women and children and in opium and other dangerous drugs"; declared the Monroe Doctrine "to be wholly outside the jurisdiction of said League of Nations"; withheld our assent to the Shantung settlement; ruled at length that no American could act in any conceivable official capacity under the League, "except with the approval of the Senate of the United States"; dared the Reparations Commission to interfere with trade between Germany and the United States, unless by act of Congress; ordained that no money should be spent for any League purpose until after an appropriation by Congress; proclaimed that no future limitation of armaments would be binding "whenever the United States is threatened with invasion or engaged in war"; reserved the right to treat as usual the nationals of Covenant-breaking states within our borders; restrained Articles 296 and 297 of the treaty from contravening "the rights of American citizens"; withheld assent from participation in the proposed International Labor Organization until Congress should so direct; refused to be bound by any action or decision of the League in which the British dominions had voted until six votes were allotted to us; and abjured any obligation to help defend others against aggression unless "the Congress, which, under the Constitution, has the sole power to declare war or authorize the employment of the military or naval forces of the United States, shall by act or joint resolution so provide."

Apart from expressing distrust of the League as a dangerous entanglement, the reservations slapped at the President throughout, giving the impression that he would do all sorts of high-handed things without the consent of Congress. The main desire of the leaders was to have the President drop the Covenant after its amended form was approved by the Senate, thus personally "killing his own child."[9] In this they did not quite succeed.

The Demand for Compromise Throttled. The Lodge reservations were defeated on November 18, 1919, by a vote of 39 for to 55 against, the fifteen bitter-enders combining with the President's supporters to make the majority. The result shook many millions of Americans to the bottom of their souls. Sensing with unerring instinct that the pitiable wastes of the war could be compensated for only by world machinery to prevent a repetition, the President had made the struggle "a war to end war" and the nations had followed him gladly. A charter of peace had been made and then slowly torn to shreds in the Senate. Now nothing was to be done. All the bloodshed and suffering, the blasted lives and the shameful squandering of the world's wealth were to go for nought, only for a fitful respite until some headstrong nation should set the world ablaze again. No informed adult who lived through November 1919 can ever forget the anguish of those weeks. It was simply incredible that the fleeting opportunity to get a world organization should be missed. It was one of those unbelievable, impossible things, the dread of which had slowly grown—but surely it would never quite occur!

It could not happen. "There is simply no acceptable alternative to a peace based on the principles of the Covenant," said the Chicago *Daily News*. "Necessity will force the Administration and the Republican friends of the Covenant to reach an agreement."[10]

There had to be a compromise that would save the substance of the League. Few thinking people did not join in that demand. In his book, published in 1925, Lodge wrote that as late as May 1, 1919, months after the Covenant had been before the public, "Most of the clergymen, the preachers of sermons, a large element of the teaching force of the universities, a large proportion of the newspaper editors, and finally the men and women who were in the habit of writing and speaking for publication, although by no means thoroughly informed, were friendly to the League as it stood and were advocating it." To this George Harvey added, from intimate knowledge, that "of all classes none was so zealous, so determined and so active as the moneyed element of New York"—the nation's economic capital. "Bankers noticeably and capitalists, though less aggressively, seemed to be literally unanimous in their advocacy."[11]

In other words, the entire leadership of the nation was strongly for the League, save only that fraction of its political leadership which controlled the United States Senate by the tainted vote of Senator Truman H. Newberry of Michigan, who was later forced out of the Senate. Attempts at compromise were imperative, efforts which proceeded during the dark days of January 1920, until the headlines presaged success. Then, as at every crisis in the long struggle, the bitter-enders cracked down. They waylaid Lodge as he approached the conference room, took him to one of their offices, and confronted him with the threats of Hiram Johnson, Borah, Knox, Moses, McCormick, Sherman, Brandegee, and Poindexter. The result of this conference with his implacables was foreordained. Lodge assured them "that there was not the slightest danger of our conceding anything that was essential or that was anything more than a change in wording."[12]

The Treaty and Reservations Defeated by Seven Votes. After this the public pressure to save something from the wreck continued so strongly that when the final vote came, March 19, 1920, only twenty of the President's stanchest supporters held out against the Lodge reservations. Their votes, plus those of fifteen bitter-enders, prevented Senate approval by the necessary two-thirds majority. The count was 49 votes for to 35 against, seven votes short of the essential two thirds.

The Reservations Thrown Aside. When the Republican national convention met in Chicago in June the irreconcilables again forbade any approval of the League. Borah made a personal attack upon ex-Senator Murray Crane of Massachusetts, accusing him of being a stooge of the House of Morgan, and threatened to bolt the ticket if the League was approved. Brandegee wept and vowed to do likewise. Lodge, who was chairman of the convention, declared that he would go to the floor and fight any effort to approve the Covenant with his own reservations.[13] They had served their purpose. A compromise plank, drafted by Elihu Root, was accordingly adopted, which condemned "the" League strongly but stood for another "association" of nations "which must be based upon justice and must provide methods which shall maintain the rule of public right by development of law and the decision of impartial courts, and which shall secure instant and general conference whenever peace shall be threatened by political action, so that the nations pledged to do and insist upon what is just and fair may exercise their influence and power for the prevention of war."

This pledge implied that judicial machinery would be enough to keep the peace, plus "instant and general conference" to mobilize the nations against any warmaker. Who should call the conference, and above all, at what stage in a chain of aggression, was not stated. The main thing was to continue to live free of the horrid political "commitments" of the League.

A Facing-Both-Ways Campaign. To stand upon this platform an ideal candidate was chosen. Warren G. Harding was a senator, regular, amiable, manageable. In astute hands he conducted a masterly campaign, from the standpoint of retaining the votes of the millions of Republicans who sincerely wanted the League of Nations. From his acceptance speech far into his presidency almost every speech he made deftly looked both ways. "One half of the speeches were for the League of Nations if you read them hastily, but if you read them with care every word of them could have been read critically as against the League of Nations. The other half were violent speeches against the League of Nations if you read them carelessly, but if you read them critically every one of them could be interpreted as in favor of the League of Nations."[14]

To clinch the votes of the pro-League half of the party Elihu Root prepared a remarkable statement which was issued on October 14, above the signatures of thirty-one of the nation's most respected Republicans. Quoting Harding's

strong utterances for a real association of nations, the statement affirmed repeatedly that the issue was "not between a
league and no league" and closed by holding out strong
hope that the League and the World Court would be revised somewhat and accepted. When millions of sorely
troubled Republicans read this statement, under the names
of the great in their party, they could and did vote both
for Harding and world organization.[15]

Wilson Destroyed. The election of 1920 focused upon
Woodrow Wilson more hatred than had ever been expressed against any American leader. The senators had done
their work well in the two whole years during which they
had appealed to every fear and suspicion that lay dormant
in the earlier Americans, at the same time mobilizing the
war-born grievances of all the newer immigrant groups. The
result was such an inferno of hate that the Springfield *Republican* questioned whether "the systematic piling up of
hatreds against a public man until a mountain of malice
disfigures the landscape" might not "finally serve as the
demonstration of his future greatness," for his most malignant enemies had "by their assaults compelled the perpetual
identification of the President's name with an ideal of international organization that is simply deathless." And when
the next great war comes, said the *Republican*, the thought
that it might have been prevented by the assassinated "Wilson League" would captivate the imagination of posterity.*

*The Springfield *Republican* (Massachusetts), October 30, 1920. No account
of this tragic struggle should fail to include a record of or tribute to the outstanding statesmanship of Senator Porter J. McCumber of North Dakota. He was
the lone Republican senator who never missed a chance to stand for the League.
His speeches and his minority report from the Committee on Foreign Relations
constitute the final, crushing evidence as to the character of the campaign
against the League. See the author's *United States and the League of Nations,*
1918–20, pp. 84–7, 148–52, 223–5, 326–8, 363–5, 396, 399. Some of the dates
of McCumber's significant utterances are: January 7, March 3, June 18, August
26, and September 10, 1919.

CHAPTER III

The Court Is Pigeonholed

IN HIS DRAFT of a League of Nations Covenant Woodrow Wilson made no provision for a world court. There was nothing in his experience, momentous as it had been, to lead him to believe that the creation of a world court would exorcise the mortal danger to civilization which the Great War had laid bare. Nevertheless he respected the desire of American and foreign advocates of judicial settlement for a court—especially the French, Italians, and small European neutrals—and Article XIV of the League Covenant required the Council to "formulate and submit to the members of the League for adoption, plans for a Permanent Court of International Justice."

In accordance with this mandate the Council created a commission of jurists to elaborate a plan for the Court, and in July 1919 Elihu Root received a cable from Colonel Edward M. House asking if he would serve. At first Root declined, since the formal consideration of the treaty was just beginning in the Senate, but a year later, after the League had twice been defeated in the Senate, he reconsidered and sailed for The Hague on June 1, 1920.[1]

A World Court Created. In his first speech in the Committee, on June 16, Root urged that the acts and resolutions of the Second Hague Conference be taken as the basis for its work. That body had been unable to constitute the proposed Permanent Court of Arbitral Justice, because of inability to agree on a plan for selecting the judges, and this was still the main problem. But Root saw that the creation of the League had solved it.[2] In collaboration with Lord Phillimore he proposed that the Council and the Assembly ballot concurrently but separately on nominees to the Court, an ordinary majority in both bodies to elect. This was, of course, the basic compromise which had enabled our own Constitution to be formed, the large states to control the House of Representatives and the small states the Senate. By the same reasoning the large nations in control of the League Council could veto any proposed judge who was objectionable to them, and the smaller nations, which were in heavy majority in the Assembly, could block any judge whose probity they doubted.

Thus the mere existence of the League solved the insoluble problem in creating a world court. The first election of judges passed off smoothly, on September 14, 1921. The Council and Assembly both elected nine judges on the first ballot; the Assembly added an American, John Bassett Moore, on the second ballot and the two soon agreed on the eleventh judge. Only on the last of the four deputy judges was there deadlock and this was soon solved by joint conference of three representatives of the two electoral bodies, a procedure which has never been necessary in any later election.[3] The Great Powers soon lost their majority on the League Council, but after their representatives numbered only four out of fifteen no difficulty developed.

In another respect also the League organization was vital to the birth of the Court. Its Secretariat worked vigorously to secure the ratification of the Protocol of Signature by the necessary twenty-five governments.[4] It is one thing to secure the signature of delegates to an international treaty, but quite another to get the ratifications of their governments back home, even when no legislative action is required.

American Participation in the Election of Judges Blocked.
Continuity with the Hague tribunal was maintained by providing that the four jurists constituting the Hague panel in each country should nominate candidates for the World Court. This system has, on the whole, worked well. Indeed, the same man has frequently been nominated by so many Hague groups that his election at Geneva was a formality. The American panel, composed of Elihu Root, Oscar Straus, John Bassett Moore, and George Gray, was not permitted to participate in the first nominations. The terror created by the fight on the League was so strong that the State Department feared to have any dealings with the League, however non-political. The Council's invitation to discuss the terms of the mandates for conquered territory was refused. The transfer of international health activities from Paris to Geneva, and of opium regulation from The Hague, was resisted. Economic statistics were anonymously contributed to the League and co-operation on arms traffic regulation withheld. For six months no mail from the League was answered and then for a time only curt mass acknowledgments went forward.[5]

It was not strange, therefore, that the League's invitation to the American Hague panel to nominate judges for the Court was lost in the State Department, and when invitations were cabled direct, even then Secretary of State Charles E. Hughes objected to nominations being made by Americans. It would involve serious risk of immediate controversy. Straus and Gray protested to Root, but the group reluctantly agreed not to nominate.[6]

"The" League Organized: "A" League Unobtainable.
After the election of 1920 the position of the pro-League Republicans was very uncomfortable. Celebrating the election returns, Harding declared that the League "is now deceased." Hughes, Hoover, Taft, and others went to see

Harding, but found George Harvey living with him and joining in their conferences. Hughes and Hoover accepted posts in the cabinet, balanced by Andrew W. Mellon and Albert B. Fall, and Harding continued to condemn "the" League and talk of "a" league. He was persuaded to propose ratification of the treaty without the Covenant, on April 12, 1921, but nothing came of that, and after many abortive attempts to find a way out of the legal state of war which still existed a separate treaty of peace was finally signed with Germany, on August 25, which reserved for us all the advantages of the Treaty of Versailles and rejected all its supposed liabilities. This got us out of the war, but left us still in a dangerous naval rivalry with both Britain and Japan. The Washington Naval Conference of 1921–22 dissolved the Anglo-Japanese Alliance and achieved a limitation of battleships, at the fatal price of putting the naval control of the Orient securely in Japan's grasp, but feelers for a new association of nations got nowhere. The membership of the League had risen to forty-six states, which were not disposed to humor the Senate by dissolving the Geneva organization. Yet the thirty-one famous Republicans had backed Harding as a way into world organization and many millions of Americans continued to be heartsore and insistent that something be done to redeem our many pledges to the dead, to the world, and to the future. The pro-League leaders knew that the negative position into which their party had been driven was dangerous from every standpoint. The election of 1924 was, moreover, approaching. Could anything be done?

A way out of the blind alley in which the Senate cabal had left us might be found by our adherence to the World Court, if the Senate would permit. To risk the wrath of the irreconcilable Thors and Wotans of the Senate, always at the eruption point, was an appalling prospect, but the overwhelming support of the nation could be counted on and it would be difficult for the embattled dozen to reject anything so traditional and so thoroughly Republicanized as the judicial approach to world order. President Harding was accordingly persuaded to propose our adherence to the Court in a message to the Senate on February 24, 1923.

Adherence to the World Court Proposed under Four Reservations. By implication the President advised the Senate that the organization of a rival court was as impractical as the construction of another League. The Court's connection with the League, of course, required reservations and these were advanced by Secretary Hughes himself, as follows:

1. That such adhesion shall not be taken to involve any legal relation on the part of the United States to the League of Nations or the assumption of any obligations by the United States under the Covenant of the League of Nations constituting Part I of the Treaty of Versailles.

2. That the United States shall be permitted to participate, through representatives designated for the purpose and upon an equality with the other states, members respectively of the Council and Assembly of the League of Nations, in any and all proceedings of either the Council or the Assembly for the election of judges or deputy judges of the Permanent Court of International Justice, or for the filling of vacancies.

3. That the United States will pay a fair share of the expenses of the Court as determined and appropriated from time to time by the Congress of the United States.

4. That the statute for the Permanent Court of International Justice adjoined to the protocol shall not be amended without the consent of the United States.

Referred to a Hostile Committee. These reservations, however, did not placate the bitter-enders and their allies with which the Committee on Foreign Relations had been packed to dispose of the League. The Committee still contained the total irreconcilables: William E. Borah, Frank Brandegee, Hiram Johnson, George Moses, and Medill McCormick, the same men who had terrorized the Republican leadership throughout the League fight. To their number could now be fairly added Henry Cabot Lodge, who had quickly abandoned his own mediatory position after the Party had been successfully held together through the long struggle in the Senate over the League. Harry S. New (Republican, Indiana) and John K. Shields (Democrat, Tennessee) were near irreconcilables.

These eight, including the chairman, could be depended on to override the other eight members: Porter J. McCumber, Frank B. Kellogg, and James Wadsworth, the three members of the dominant party who did believe in international co-operation; Gilbert Hitchcock, Claude Swanson, Altee Pomerene, and Key Pittman, Democrats—all moderate, reasonable men. Only John Sharp Williams of Mississippi was fiery enough to meet the tactics of the battery of eruptive bitter-enders.

Death and defeat at the polls removed some of the diehards in the twelve years during which the Committee was to operate on the World Court proposals, but the original hard core of obstruction was sufficient to dominate it until the end of the period. Lodge and Brandegee died, but G. W. Pepper and Henrik Shipstead took their places. In 1925 James A. Reed of Missouri became a member and continued in the next Congress after the hardly less irreconcilable David A. Reed of Pennsylvania had been added. Other opposition recruits were: Arthur R. Robinson, Indiana, Robert M. La Follette, Jr., Wisconsin, Arthur H. Vandenberg, Michigan, and Otis Glenn, Illinois.

Was It a League Court? In 1923 the Committee thus constituted promptly termed the Court a "League Court" and sat down upon Mr. Hughes's proposition that we adhere to it. This led the Court's proponents to commit the mistake of arguing that the Court's connection with the League was so remote that it was now an independent entity, standing upon its own statute. This was technically true. Separate action by the governments had approved the statute and the independence of the judges was not questioned outside of the United States. On the other hand, the Court could not have been created in the absence of the League and it would be of no avail if the League failed in its crucial task of preventing other world wars. The Court was a useful and necessary adjunct of the League, but everything depended on the success of the main body. Theoretically, the Court could call upon the governments to set up new machinery for paying its expenses and filling its vacancies, continuing in being after the fall of the League. But apart from dispensing justice to a cemetery, the Court in such a situation would be no stronger than the political machinery back of it.

In *The Constitution at the Cross Roads,* Edward A. Harriman wrote that "it is a legal impossibility to have any true international court which shall not be a court of the League of Nations, for the simple reason that there is no other international government which can entrust such a body with the administration of justice." In the legal sense, he continued, those who oppose a League Court are opposed to any real court. They desire that controversies shall be settled "by an impartial body of jurists." Friends of the League argued that the Court is such a body, but an "impartial body of jurists is not a court, but a mere tribunal of arbitration. A court is a body in a government, which administers justice in accordance with the law of that government. Its judges are the officers of that government."[7]

This was sound common sense, but it made no impression on Senator Borah, who took his usual high and confusing position. He explained to a New York audience, on March 19, that he was for "a" court, but not this one. He objected to the World Court because the League Council and Assembly had rejected the compulsory jurisdiction that Mr. Root had persuaded the Commission of Jurists to propose. The League bodies had considered this clause with great care and had concluded that it was in conflict with Article XII of the Covenant, which bound the members of the League to a different procedure for the pacific settlement of disputes.[8] Borah lamented the lack of compulsory jurisdiction and the inability of the Court to enforce its decisions. He would support a court patterned after our Supreme Court, but there must be no armies and navies back of it, only public opinion.[9]

On May 3 Senator King of Utah tried to obtain action, but his motion was defeated without debate, 49 to 24. Only one Republican voted for consideration, though on May 20 the New York *Times* made a poll of the Senate which indicated that 73 senators were for the Court, 37 Republicans and 36 Democrats. The heavy majority for entering the Court did not mean that we would do so, commented the *Times* editorially the next day. The large supply of lethal weapons and poison gas which the Foreign Relations Committee had accumulated for use against President Wilson would hold out long enough to do President Harding's measure to death. "Of course," continued the *Times*:

Chairman Lodge and the other Republican members of the Committee will profess an eager desire to support the Administration; but gentlemen of their weight and dignity cannot be asked to move in a hurry. The Senate will meet in December, but it would be too much to expect the Committee on Foreign Relations to come to a conclusion before the Christmas holidays. By that time they will scarcely have got their ponderous intellects fairly in motion. Later will come the period of high debate within the Committee. There will be profound historical and legal disquisitions to be listened to week after week. Then the era of amendments and reservations will set in. These will all have to be studied down to their minutest verbal shadings. If the Committee gets around to making a report to the Senate by the middle of February, it will be almost a miracle of speed.

The climate in the Senate favorable to the Court was disturbed on June 21, when President Harding executed his invariable switch back to the other side. He had pursued this technique so long that it was a part of him, even if his habit of yielding to the bitter-enders had not become fixed. In his message to the Senate on February 24 he had said that the four reservations would leave the United States "wholly free from any legal relation to the League." But on June 21, in St. Louis, he declared that the Court must be "so constituted as to appear and to be, in theory and practice, in form and in substance, beyond shadow of doubt, a World Court and not a League Court." He preferred the "Court's complete independence of the League."[10]

Harding died soon afterward and was succeeded by President Calvin Coolidge, who in his first annual message to Congress, on December 3, 1923, urged favorable consideration of the Court, saying: "As I wish to see a court established, and as the proposal presents the only practical plan on which many nations have ever agreed, though it may not meet every desire, I therefore commend it to the favorable consideration of the Senate." The Committee, however, was not impressed.

Separation from the League Proposed. To induce it to move, Senator Lenroot of Wisconsin introduced a resolution on December 10 proposing that all states accredited to The Hague be permitted to join the Court and that a new electoral scheme be devised. Group A, to be composed of seven large nations, would receive the power to elect judges possessed by the League Council. Group B, including all other states, would inherit the Assembly's share in the elections. Other provisions completed the separation of the Court from the League.

It may not be easy for an American even now to sense the full effrontery of that proposal. To propitiate a band of American senators who had done all that they could to prevent the creation of the League, and who had finally prevented our participation in it, Lenroot solemnly proposed that fifty-four governments and peoples which now belonged to the League confess publicly that there was something dangerous and unclean about it, by setting up a pure Council and Assembly into which Americans might enter momentarily, for a rigidly limited purpose. What self-respecting government or people would consider such a proposal?

A few days after it was made Senator Lodge explained to his constituents that he was "thoroughly in favor of a World Court," but it must be "a true World Court and not involved in any way with the League of Nations." He was not in favor of the existing Court unless separated from the League. The best way to get a "true" Court would be to take the old Hague tribunal and make it permanent.[11]

A Hearing Finally Held. Five months more passed, while public impatience grew. But Chairman Lodge protested twice during April that the Committee was terribly busy. As to the Court, "that does not require immediate action, because we have now fifty individual arbitration treaties" and there was also the Hague tribunal. But public pressure could no longer be completely ignored. On April 8, 1924, the Committee received from one group of prominent citizens a demand which asked sharply: "Are we to understand that it is the purpose of the Committee to repudiate the recommendations of both President Harding and President Coolidge in this vital matter? Certainly you cannot plead lack of time. The proposal has been in the hands of your Committee almost fourteen months. As citizens addressing their public servants it is our right to request that some public explanation be made of your failure to act."

Some kind of hearing could no longer be avoided, so a subcommittee was appointed to hold one. The resolution providing for it did not ask for any recommendation or report. It was merely to let the pro-Court people talk. This group of five, dominated by anti-Leaguers George Wharton Pepper, Brandegee, and Shipstead, met on April 30 and heard former Attorney General Wickersham say: "We cannot decently urge the creation of such a Court as this upon the rest of the world through a long series of years and then repudiate the Court when they consent to it, unless we offer some adequate reason."

Scoring Lodge's excuse for delay, Bishop Charles H. Brent, chief chaplain of the A.E.F., warned that "unless our government provides a moral substitute for war, as far as in it lies, a vast proportion of our citizenry are presently going to find themselves in the predicament of being opposed to war as an arbiter in international disputes, but without any provision being made for an adequate substitute of a peaceful and orderly character."[12]

After a dozen similar appeals Senator Claude Swanson of Virginia introduced, on May 5, a resolution proposing to adhere to the Court under the Harding-Hughes terms. This Democratic initiative led Senator Lodge to present, on May 8, a plan which ignored the World Court entirely. It requested the President to call a third Hague conference to create a court free in every respect from the League of Nations, a proposal which the Hartford *Times* characterized as "a piece of colossal impudence toward the many nations that have put the World Court into operation, and an affront to the intelligence of the American people."[13]

Painless Divorce from the League Advocated. Since the Lodge plan could not be considered seriously, and since the Lenroot plan for brutally cutting the Court apart from the League had fallen flat, Senator George Wharton Pepper of Pennsylvania essayed, on May 22, an elaborate plan for painlessly divorcing the Court and the League. Pepper proposed a scheme under which the Council and Assembly could simply adjourn as League organs and be called to order in response to a call from the secretary-general of the old Hague tribunal. Then an American could walk into each body, vote for judges of the Court, and walk out again, uncontaminated by the political leprosy of the League. Having publicly admitted that they were normally engaged in nefarious business, the representatives of fifty-five nations would then reassemble and continue to transact the affairs of the League.

This proposal was actually voted out of the Committee, on May 22, after the Swanson resolution had been rejected 10 to 8, though some senators voted for it only to get something before the Senate. Then another perfunctory move to create an impression of activity having been made, the Isle of Pines Treaty was called up by Senator Borah and given the right of way. This venerable relic had been gathering dust in the committee pigeonholes since 1904.

A few days later the national conventions of both parties endorsed the Court, and Coolidge, its advocate, received an overwhelming popular vote. But the election did not lead to early entry into the Court. Lodge had died, but Borah sat ominously in his chair. On January 25, 1925, he warned the Committee that all other legislation would be held up if the Court was taken up at that session, and it was not.

The Abandonment of Subterfuges Urged by Coolidge. In his inaugural address on March 4 Coolidge spoke out sharply for the Court, in words which might have applied as truly to the League. Said the President:

"Where great principles are involved, where great movements are under way which promise much for the welfare of humanity by reason of the very fact that many other nations have given such movements their actual support, we ought not to withhold our own sanction because of any small and unessential difference, but only upon the ground of the most important and compelling fundamental reasons. We cannot barter away our independence or our sovereignty, but we ought to engage in no refinement of logic, no sophistries, and no subterfuges to argue away the undoubted duty of this country by reason of the might of its numbers, the power of its resources, and its position of leadership in the world, actively and comprehensively to signify its approval and to bear its full share of the responsibility of a candid and disinterested attempt at the establishment of a tribunal for the administration of even-handed justice between nation and nation. The weight of our enormous influence must be cast upon the side of a reign not of force, but of law and trial, not by battle, but by reason."

This forthright statement led at last to the fixing of a date when consideration of the Swanson resolution would begin in the Senate, but not at once—nine months later, on December 17, 1925, two years and ten months after the Harding-Hughes proposal.

The impotence of the American people to affect the bitter-enders who bestrode the Court proposal was described in an address at Yale University, on December 3, 1925, by Homer Cummings, later Attorney General of the United States, in biting but accurate terms. Said Cummings: "What stands in the way of our entry into the World Court?

"Not the American people; not the executive or judicial branch of our government; not the House of Representatives; not even the Senate of the United States; but only a small, belligerent, irreconcilable group of senators who hold a strategic position on the Committee on Foreign Relations and whose pride of opinion is more important to them than the peace of the world. They take counsel of their fears and prejudices. They convert the Senate chamber into a veritable clinic of political obsessions and mental complexes. They cling with pestilential persistence to the husk of an idea from which long since all substance has departed.

"The real and underlying objection on the part of the irreconcilables is that the World Court is called into being by the Fourteenth Article of the Covenant of the League of Nations. . . . They fear that the Court will work and they fear the consequences of that success. They fear to lose an issue; they fear to lose their own prestige as wise and cautious leaders. . . .

"They would tear the Court statute to tatters and throw its fragments in the face of the civilized world if they could. . . . Under the shelter of the constitutional requirement of a two-thirds vote, aided by their control of the Committee on Foreign Relations, and abetted by the archaic rules of the Senate, they will seek to kill the project by protracted debate and by confusing and nullifying amendments and reservations."

During all this time discussion of the Court did not rise to the level of argument. It takes two sides to make an argument and the opposition contented itself mainly with pure obstruction and with impossible, insulting proposals for the divorce of the Court from the League. The men who had smashed our participation in the League continued on the assumption that the people had endorsed their action so completely in 1920 that all they had to do to defeat the Court was to pin the League taint on it.

Public Opinion Overwhelmingly for the Court. Actually national opinion was almost unanimous in favor of the Court. Both political parties stood squarely for it. The House of Representatives voted for adherence, on March 3, 1925, 301 to 28. The most powerful national organizations in the land all advocated entry—the National Association of Manufacturers, the United States Chamber of Commerce, the American Legion, the American Federation of Labor, and the National Republican Club. The American Bar Association voted for going in, as did the League of Women Voters and the American Association of University Women, the General Federation of Women's Clubs, and the Federation of Business and Professional Women's Clubs.

Religious bodies voting for entry included: the Presbyterian General Assembly, the National Council of Congregational Churches, the Federal Council of Churches of Christ, the World's Sunday School Association, the United Christian Endeavor Societies, the General Conference of the Methodist Episcopal Church, the Northern Baptist Convention, the House of Bishops of the Protestant Episcopal Church, the Church Peace Union, the American Unitarian Association, the Synod of the Reformed Presbyterian Church, the General Conference of Friends, the International Convention of Disciples of Christ, the United Presbyterian Church of North America, the Universalist General Convention, and scores of lesser religious bodies.

Some fifteen state fraternal orders also passed pro-Court resolutions in addition to many educational and racial associations and all of the great Jewish organizations. The most striking expressions of opinion, however, came from business and professional bodies. On October 18, 1925, the American Foundation released a list of fifty organizations which had endorsed the Court, including almost every conceivable type of association. The same Foundation also surveyed the press and found that, of 1042 leading daily newspapers, 865, or 83 per cent, had expressed themselves as favoring adherence; 114, or 11 per cent, were opposed and 62, or 6 per cent, had taken no stand. The opposition included the twenty-two Hearst papers, the New York *Sun*, the Kansas City *Star*, the Chicago *Tribune*, and the Washington *Post*. This group in general opposed the step as a backdoor entry into the League, though a considerable number of the 114 opposed took that position on the ground that joining the Court was too small a step, merely a smoke screen to cover our failure to enter the League.[14]

"The Smallest Possible Step." Joining the Court was the smallest possible step we could take, said Secretary of Commerce Herbert Hoover. "The Court," he continued, "is not the total solution of international co-operation for peace, for the great field of political action as distinguished from judicial action remains unsolved, but this step is sound and sure. It is the minimum possible step in eliminating the causes of war."[15]

This was a correct appraisal of our situation. Our adherence to the World Court would have very little practical importance. The Court was already open to us, if we chose to use it. Our "belonging" to it might make us a little readier to submit weighty cases to it, but no government of a Great Power was ready to submit the vital issues which lead to war to judicial settlement. These would be settled by the League of Nations or war would return again. The success of the League was the burning, crucial issue, upon which everything depended.

The value of our adherence to the Court would be moral. If it was a step into the League it would have great significance. If it was not, it would be for us a deceptive substitute for the only international machinery which could avert another and more terrible holocaust. This was as crystal-clear then as it is now. "There can be no confidence in the continuity of our civilization," warned Mr. Hoover in 1925, "unless preventive safeguards can be established."[16]

CHAPTER IV

A Fifth Reservation

As THE TIME for Senate consideration of the Court proposal at last approached it was necessary for the objectors to be ready with a great danger to the Republic. Our people were so overwhelmingly for the Court that it could not be defeated outright. The never-failing strategy of destructive reservations which would kill under the guise of doing good would have to be applied. Nearly three years of campaigning by the isolationists, while they sat upon the proposal in committee, had failed to stir the hoped-for wave of hatred against the Court. On the contrary, as December 17, 1925, approached, mass meetings in its favor were held in dozens of cities.[1] But the opposition was ready. It had gradually been developing the advisory-opinion function of the Court as the great danger.

An Alleged Danger Discovered. The executive authorities of every government often require expert advice on knotty legal questions. President George Washington first turned to the United States Supreme Court and, being rebuffed, he resorted to his own Attorney General. In our states a number of supreme courts accepted the function and seven of them still discharge it: Massachusetts, New Hampshire, Maine, Rhode Island, Florida, Colorado, and South Dakota.[2] The giving of a hundred and fifty advisory opinions by the Massachusetts Supreme Court, during a hundred and fifty years, has not lowered its dignity, but the assignment of the advisory-opinion function of the League system to the World Court gave the isolationists their opening. It enabled them to make the only charge which would have a chance of success—that the Court was "political." During their two-year war on the League they had finally made that a witch word. Nothing was so bad as international "politics," and vice versa, everything else tended to be good, or at least better. International economics was all right; the more the merrier, even when it added up to collecting ten billions of war debts while refusing to accept them in goods and continuously lending American goods to the debtors—and myriads of new ones—with which they purchased gold or dollars to send to us. Likewise, international organization of a judicial nature was accounted different from the horrid "politics," which soiled and tainted everything it touched—until the World Court was close to approval. Then a political taint was pinned on it.

The League Council, it was said, should get its legal advice somewhere else. And the Council did ask its own legal experts for advice on purely legal and constitutional points which did not involve international disputes. This is a point not generally understood. It was only in cases when interpretations of international law were involved in disputes between national states that the deliberation of the World Court was desired—and required.

The wisdom of giving the advisory-opinion function to the Court was amply vindicated by the productive use to which the function was put. The League Council often found itself blocked by legal questions in its efforts to settle international disputes, and several serious controversies, of the kind which lead to war, were settled after the Court had rendered an advisory opinion. On the other hand, only one of the cases settled by judgment was likely to lead to war and in no judgment case was public opinion aroused, as in several of the advisory-opinion cases. It is the opinion of Manley O. Hudson, the leading authority on the World Court, that "through its advisory opinions, rather than through its judgments, the Court has made its most direct and significant contributions to the maintenance of peace."[8]

Advisory Opinions Conservatively Given. The allocation of the advisory-opinion function to the Court forced that body to decide early what procedure it would use. It was soon settled that the same procedure used in giving judgments would be adhered to as closely as possible; public hearings and arguments, careful study of all aspects, and the reading of the opinion in open court. The next year, on April 23, 1923, the Court declined to give an advisory opinion on the Eastern Karelia dispute between Finland and Soviet Russia, because Russia had refused to give her consent. It was established then that no secret opinions would be given, and no state's interests prejudiced by an opinion given without its consent.

Judge John Bassett Moore led the Court in arriving at these decisions, but he was not satisfied. There had been a minority of judges who took the other view, in both cases. Moore was opposed, moreover, to the whole advisory-opinion function. In a memorandum of February 18, 1922, he had argued that giving advisory opinions was not a function of a court, that they would diminish its judicial business and reduce the development of international law. He felt that it was incompatible with the general character and purpose of the Court to be required to give advisory opinions which could be rejected. He contended that Article XIV of the Covenant was permissive and that it was not desirable to encourage the asking of advisory opinions by making any special provision for them.[4]

No Danger Seen by Coolidge. Knowing where the main

attack would come, President Coolidge said in his 1925 annual message to Congress:

"It does not seem that the authority to give advisory opinions interferes with the independence of the Court. Advisory opinions in and of themselves are not harmful, but may be used in such a way as to be very beneficial because they undertake to prevent injury rather than merely afford a remedy after the injury has been done. It is a principle that only implies that the Court shall function when proper application is made to it. Deciding the question involved upon issues submitted for an advisory opinion does not differ materially from deciding the question involved upon issues submitted by contending parties. Up to the present time the Court has given an advisory opinion when it judged it had jurisdiction and refused to give one when it judged it did not have jurisdiction. Nothing in the work of the Court has yet been an indication that this is an impairment of its independence or that its practice differs materially from the giving of like opinions under the authority of the constitutions of several of our states.

"No provision of the statute seems to me to give this Court any authority to be a political rather than judicial court. We have brought cases in this country before courts which, when they have been adjudged to be political, have been thereby dismissed. It is not improbable that political questions will be submitted to this Court, but again up to the present time the Court has refused to pass on political questions and our support will undoubtedly have a tendency to strengthen it in that refusal."

Then followed sound words of wisdom on the first requisite for international co-operation.

"If we are going to support any court, it would not be one that we have set up alone or which reflects only our ideals. Other nations have their customs and their institutions, their thoughts and their methods of life. If a court is going to be international, its composition will have to yield to what is good in all these various elements. Neither will it be possible to support a court which is exactly perfect, or under which we assume absolutely no obligations. If we are seeking that opportunity, we might as well declare that we are opposed to supporting any court. If any agreement is made, it will be because it undertakes to set up a tribunal which can do more of the things these other nations wish to have done."

The President concluded with this blunt statement of truth: "Like all others engaged in the war, whatever we said, as a matter of fact we joined an alliance, we became a military power, we impaired our independence. We have more at stake than anyone else in avoiding a repetition of that calamity."

A Reservation Conceded: We Are "in No Manner Bound." When December 17 came, Senator Swanson endeavored to head off the advisory-opinion assault by adding a fifth reservation to the four originally proposed by Secretary Hughes. It read:

"That the United States shall be in no manner bound by any advisory opinion of the Permanent Court of International Justice not rendered pursuant to a request in which it, the United States, shall expressly join in accordance with the statute for the said Court adjoined to the protocol of signature of the same to which the United States shall become signatory."

On December 21 Senator Thomas J. Walsh, Democrat, of Montana, one of the ablest lawyers in the Senate, discussed the advisory-opinion issue, maintaining that this function was much better safeguarded in the Court than in our own states, where arguments were not required. Nor was it a weighty criticism that no judgment was entered. That was true of nine tenths of the cases decided by the Supreme Court. The complaint that the League had emasculated the Court by refusing to give it compulsory jurisdiction came strangely from men who continually feared entanglement of some kind. Nor was the claim that the Monroe Doctrine could be abolished by an advisory opinion valid. We had never tried to prevent other American nations from resorting to any tribunal of their own choosing. How could we begin now?[5]

The opposition, however, insisted that nothing must be left to chance in the future. On the same day Senator George Wharton Pepper proposed to stiffen Reservation 5 as follows: (1) that the United States declare its understanding that the present practice of the Court in giving no secret or confidential advice was to be permanent—we must state in no uncertain terms that we were adhering to a court, not a conclave; (2) we should pledge the other signatory powers to the principle that the policy laid down by the Court in the Eastern Karelia case of refusing to give an advisory opinion when one of the parties refused the jurisdiction of the Court was not to be reversed; and (3) instead of merely declaring that we would not be bound by any advisory opinion which we had not joined in submitting we should go further and require "that there shall be no advisory opinion on any matter directly affecting the United States unless the United States shall have consented that the Court take jurisdiction."[6]

Everything must be nailed down for all time. It was the rule of the Court that its proceedings should be public. Why not, then, bind the Court never to do otherwise? Likewise with the rule of consent to jurisdiction laid down in the Eastern Karelia case. It was most unlikely that this precedent would ever be reversed, but since the possibility existed it must be forestalled. This perfectionist line of argument always appeals to many senators in considering treaties. If a thing is conceivable it must be legislated against.

Senator Bruce of Maryland cautioned that the Court "be not so transformed by our reservations that the nations which are now members of that Court will be unwilling to admit us into it; and in weighing the possibility of that result, we should not forget that the other great civilized powers of the earth have lost to a considerable extent their eager desire that we should become a party to the concert they have so successfully established."[7]

This lone warning of what was most likely to occur fell on deaf ears. Most senators were still under the illusion that any terms they might require would be accepted. The opponents of the Court began to insist on the inadequacy of Reservation 5. It did not put us on an equality with the other Great Powers, urged Senator Williams of Missouri, since they had seats on the Council and could by their single votes prevent the submission of any question to the Court for an advisory opinion. Said Borah, on January 14, 1926, "We could not object, because we are not on the Council, and we could not shape the question, because we are not on the Council, and yet we would have all the influence and power of the Court thrown against us in our absence and notwithstanding our refusal to consent."[8]

"*Madness.*" Calling out the names of the World Court judges was a device used repeatedly by the opposition. Senator Fernald of Maine protested against our approaching a Court composed of eleven judges, ten of whose names no American could correctly pronounce. Of the eleven judges just one was an American, and of the deputy judges "Not an American! Of the four not a single American!" Senator James A. Reed of Missouri not only asked the Senate how they would like to wait for decisions on American questions by Dionisco Anzilotti, or Antonio Sánchez de Bustamante, but read pages of the names of League of Nations delegates. Reed conjured the League into a hostile alliance against the United States, a result he and his fellow irreconcilables had done their best to produce. We would "combine against ourselves if we should recognize this power, the force of all the fifty-five nations that make up the League. This, sir, is madness. This, sir, I unhesitatingly say, is disloyalty," said Reed, and cried, "Tell me this is not a league of offense against the United States! Tell me that it does not exist!" Borah also saw the League evolving into a "gigantic world military machine."

These were dark days for the formerly triumphant anti-Leaguers. They feared that they were going to lose out after all. Said Hiram Johnson gloomily: "We are going into the Court because we are going to be taken into the League of Nations. It follows just as absolutely as night follows day. There can be no escape from it." We were about to be entangled, warned Borah, on the eighteenth. The power to call for advisory opinions created "a definite permanent association with a political institution."[9]

Appeals to Sanity. These demands that we be aloof, exclusive, trusting no foreigners, were countered occasionally, especially by Senators McLean, Republican, of Connecticut, and Tyson, Democrat, of Tennessee. Said McLean:

"If we want to live in a civilized world, I think it is high time we screwed our courage up to a point that will enable us to treat our neighbors in a civilized manner. We know that for the purposes of trade and the distribution of good and bad advice the earth today is no larger than was the District of Columbia a hundred years ago. While trade may not follow the flag, we know that politics will follow trade as surely as noontide follows the dawn. With our goods in every port and our debits and credits in every court and countinghouse, we might as well try to keep the Mississippi River out of the Gulf of Mexico as to try to keep politics out of our foreign relations."[10]

Near the close of the debate Senator Tyson showed clearly that he understood that power and responsibility go together, saying:

"We of the United States of America say that we are the greatest nation in the world; that we are the richest nation in the world;

that we have the greatest resources of any nation in the world and that none of the nations of the world can come here and attack us; in fact, it is said that all the nations of the world might attack us at one time and they could not overcome us. I agree to every single one of those statements; and yet we are so afraid of ourselves, so afraid to take a chance, so afraid to do what even the smallest nations of the world have done, that it seems to me we have no reason to be so self-satisfied; that we cannot feel any pride in being the greatest, the most powerful, the strongest nation, because we will not take any chance of getting hurt. Why all this greatness? Why all this wealth? Why all this strength? Is it the destiny of one so great to be so small? Has God blessed us with riches, empowered us with strength, and endowed us with greatness that we may be of all nations the least and the last to comprehend his blessing of 'Peace on earth; good will to men'?"

Cloture Voted. As argument became exhausted several efforts were made to secure another year of delay. On January 12 Senator Shipstead of Minnesota introduced a resolution suggesting that the Committee on Foreign Relations gather data on every aspect of the negotiations surrounding the establishment of the Court. On the fifteenth Senator Cole Blease of South Carolina began a filibuster, making no effort to hide the fact. A tax-reduction measure was very much desired by conservative senators before the short session ended on March 4. It was hoped therefore that a filibuster would force the Court proposal aside. On the nineteenth Blease offered a resolution to fix the date for a vote on the eighth day of December 1926. However, the majority did not surrender to these tactics. Cloture was successfully invoked, by the necessary two-thirds majority, on January 25.

Stiffening Demanded by Judge Moore. In the meantime the opposition had won the fight by convincing the majority that the fifth reservation must be further stiffened. For this achievement they were indebted to the powerful and in all probability decisive support of the only American judge on the World Court, Judge John Bassett Moore. When he appeared in Washington one evening before a group of some twenty senators and advised that the United States take an absolute veto on the hearing of advisory opinions there was no one to refute him. His impressive personality, his prestige as the greatest living authority on international law, his unique experience as the only American who had been in the bosom of the World Court, all combined to silence opposition to a drastic stiffening of the fifth reservation.

This was the more the case after Senator Borah introduced a memorandum into the *Congressional Record*, on January 18, 1926, which everyone attributed to Moore. Though some sense of propriety prevented Moore from signing the document and denied Borah permission to say who wrote it, no one could think of any other "well-known international jurist . . . in official life."

The Moore memorandum refused to trust the good sense of the Court to uphold the sound precedent of the Eastern Karelia case. It had been set "only by a majority of 7 to 4, so that a difference of two votes would have turned the scale the other way. Such a difference might easily occur in another case. Wholly apart from the possibility of two of the majority judges shifting their position, the absence of two of them and the substitution of two deputies might produce the same result." When to these possibilities was added "the formal reservation made by the Council" and "what has occurred since" (probably the Mosul case), the conclusion was drawn that the Eastern Karelia precedent could never have been accepted as a sufficient safeguard for the future "by any prudent statesman."

This reproof to Secretary Hughes was supported by the assertion that the issue at stake was "too vital, too far-reaching, too profound." It was "simply whether the United

States, which is not a member of the League of Nations, shall, in adhering to the Court, put itself in a position of national inferiority by omitting to assure to itself a right of self-protection similar to that which other Great Powers, members of the League, possess."

Senator Swanson, too, had been equally remiss, said the memorandum. Swanson's fifth reservation was "worse than useless," because it accepted the right of the Court to give advisory opinions in which we were concerned, while each of the Great Powers on the Council could block the *submission* of questions to the Court. Upon what principle should the United States "renounce the right of self-protection in like circumstances? Strange as it may seem," continued the memorandum, "the proposal to denude the United States of this right of self-protection is made solely in the United States. There is not the slightest reason to suppose that any other country would have the hardihood either to propose to the United States such an act of self-immolation, or to deny the request of the United States to be treated as an equal."

For once the Senate's reservation makers had been too meek and mild, leaving their country in a position of dangerous inferiority. Nothing should be left to the natural and powerful desire of the judges to build a permanent institution and to avoid offense to powerful, touchy governments. The judges and all their successors should be bound for all time now. Let the Senate require, proposed the international jurist:

"That, in acting upon requests for advisory opinions, the Court shall not, under any circumstances, depart from the essential rules guiding its activity as a judicial tribunal but shall give notice and open hearings to all interested parties, and shall in such case freely determine, in the exercise of its own judgment, whether it can, in keeping with its judicial character, properly answer the question put to it, and what shall be the nature and form of its response;

that in no case shall the Court give any confidential advice but shall announce its opinions publicly, together with the opinions of dissenting judges; that the Court shall not give an opinion on a question to which the United States is a party without the consent of the United States; and that the United States disclaims all responsibility for any opinion on any question to the submission of which the United States was not a party."[11]

These were good rules. They had been adopted by the Court under Judge Moore's able championing, but it did not follow that a new member could successfully approach the Court, gingerly demanding that these maxims be bound on it for eternity. The jurist was confident that no other country "would have the hardihood" to deny us this prescription for gaining "equality," but to the other members of the Court it was bound to appear as something more than that. They were, in effect, asked to admit that the United States could not be safe from their nefarious attentions unless these guarantees of good behavior were riveted on the Court. The Moore memorandum really proved that the Court was too risky a place for Uncle Sam.

The senators in charge of the Court proposal could not go as far as the memorandum demanded, but they felt compelled to adopt its key point. The opposition had been hinting frequently that the advisory-opinion procedure would be used to cast doubt upon the validity of the Monroe Doctrine. Maybe, too, the League Council would induce the Court to say that our high tariffs were excessive, or that our exclusion of oriental immigrants was inequitable. Such opinions would have no legal force, but wouldn't they be embarrassing? Above all there were the war debts. Surely, said the isolationists, our creditors will gang up on us through an advisory opinion that will be used as moral justification for not paying their debts.

Another fear that was played upon was the possibility

that the repudiated debts of several Southern states might be brought up. About $75,000,000 of bonds issued by the "carpet bag" governments of Reconstruction days were involved, and interest charges four times as large. The possible raising of these claims was forbidden by a reservation introduced by Senator Overman of North Carolina, which insured the support of the Southern Democrats for a stiffened fifth reservation.

The Reservations Expanded. These alleged perils had been forestalled, insofar as they could eventuate in any practical effect, by the original terms of the fifth reservation. We would not be "in any manner bound" by any advisory opinion which we had not joined in requesting. But by now that was not sufficient. Judge Moore had convinced the senators that we must not only refuse to be bound, but to be embarrassed, in any conceivable circumstance. He was therefore called in by Senators Swanson and Walsh and the fifth reservation was stiffened to require "that the Court shall not render any advisory opinion except publicly, after due notice to all states adhering to the Court and to all interested states, and after public hearing or opportunity for hearing given to any state concerned; nor shall it without the consent of the United States entertain any request for an advisory opinion touching any dispute or question in which the United States has or claims an interest."[12]

No "Intruding, Entangling, or Interfering." Then the hoary reservation of the Hague Conferences was added.[13] It was proclaimed again that nothing could induce the United States to depart from "its traditional policy of not intruding upon, interfering with, or entangling itself in the political questions or policy of internal administration of any foreign state." And no one should assume that there was any "relinquishment by the United States of its traditional attitude toward purely American questions."

No Case to the Court without a Two-Thirds Vote of the Senate. When this ritual had been included in the resolution one might have supposed that not even a microscopic chance remained that the mighty United States could be intruded upon, interfered with, or entangled politically by the sly machinations of the wicked foreign nations, operating through the Permanent Court of International Justice. But to reinsure reinsurance, still another reservation required that recourse to the Court "can be had only by agreement thereto through general or special treaties concluded between the parties to the dispute." This ban, relic of the placid years before the Great War had shattered the illusion that the peaceful settlement of disputes was a luxury, once more warned all secretaries of state not to send any dispute to judicial settlement without the express authorization of two thirds of the Senate.

"Adherence" Voted. When all these fortifications had been set up against the sordid world, the Senate voted to permit adherence to the World Court, on January 27, 1926, by a vote of 76 to 17, almost three years from the time when that step was first proposed.

The day before the final vote Senator Frederick H. Gillett, Republican, of Massachusetts, put the step about to be taken into its proper perspective. He told the Senate plainly that the original reservations were unnecessary and the stiffening of the fifth reservation superfluous. Without it there was no reason to fear that any advisory opinion would injure us. He had not favored giving the Court the advisory-opinion function, but experience had justified the experiment, enhancing the reputation of the Court. Sound rules governing the giving of advisory opinions had been adopted and there was exceedingly small probability that they would be reversed. Taking pride in the Court as they did, the judges would be as slow to offend any great nation as the Council would be to invite loss of prestige by asking the Court to reverse its well-accepted practices.

Both sides, said Gillett, had exaggerated the importance of our adherence to the Court. It was only a first step and a short one. The real goal, the acceptance of compulsory jurisdiction by all nations, was far enough away, but it was our clear duty to take the next step toward ending war and let the next generation do likewise, with confidence that "sometime a method will be found which will end all war."

"*A Surly Nod.*" Here was the statesman's outlook that had been missing from the hue and cry to get for us a bomb-proof nook in the World Court, so well fortified that no misguided judge or member of the League Council could ever cause us the slightest concern about our wealth and privileges. The Senate, said the Springfield *Republican* on February 4, 1926, "sulkily gives a distant nod of recognition to the Court," and the Des Moines *Register* concluded that "our actual entry into the World Court, if the nations finally accept us on the terms we name, will be so tentative that unless we ourselves ignore the reservations or abandon them we shall not really contribute much."

Plunging through the foam of reservations to the cold waters of the great problem beneath, the *Register* continued:

What this debate has brought out plainer than ever is the want of a sense of responsibility on our part for future world order. No real emphasis has been put on our part in securing an international code, and an international tribunal to set up civil adjudication of international disputes. We treat the matter as though we were doing the other peoples a special favor by consenting to have anything to do with a World Court. It is nothing to us and everything to them.

Those who really believe in the World Court are just the other way around. They feel that it is far more to America's interest and to the interest of the English-speaking peoples to secure world order than to the interest of any other people or peoples. It is our part in world affairs to have civil adjustment in the place of violent outbreaks. That has been our talent as a people and that is our program. We cannot function in a world of disorder and wars. We should lead, not follow, in the matter of international code, of international court, of international council table.

How desperately true these words would be later, after the League of Nations had been successfully defied by gangster empires on both sides of us! Writing on January 29, 1926, the editor of the *Register* did not foresee the gnawing terror that struck our hearts after the fall of France in 1940, but he spoke warning truth which was open to everybody while the Senate gravely sought for us theoretically perfect protection against the all-too-weak infant institutions of world government, which instead of menacing us soon languished and died. While the Senate dallied for three years with the World Court, as a cat does with a mouse, the precious moment in which the world might have been organized against a return of international anarchy was passing with the speed of an airplane.*

*Commenting on the remarkable obstructive power of the Committee majority, when led by an able, determined chairman, Eleanor Dennison says: "The ability of Lodge and Borah to delay action for three years on a measure which had the approval of a large part of the electorate, the Administration and the Senate itself is astonishing," and she adds that Borah announced in a radio address the day after the vote in the Senate that the fight was not over. He would make it an issue "in every precinct in the United States." Eleanor Dennison, *The Senate Foreign Relations Committee* (Stanford Press, 1942), p. 122.

Borah was not deterred by finding himself on the lonely end of a 76–17 vote in the Senate. What had been done before could be done again. The fight had just begun—as indeed it had.

CHAPTER V

The Reaction of the Powers

THE ADOPTION of the stiffened fifth reservation raised three important questions: (1) would it give "equality" to the United States and the League members; (2) was unanimous consent in the Council necessary and advisable in asking for advisory opinions; and (3) would the members of the Court accept the United States under the conditions laid down?

The Quest for "Equality." Actually the United States could not stand on a basis of perfect equality with the permanent members of the Council unless it accepted full membership in that body. The Council members had upon their shoulders the heavy responsibility of settling international disputes, both before they led to war and after they had done so. The controversies with which the Council had wrestled seem puny to us now—the Aaland Islands, Upper Silesia, Albania's boundaries, Vilna, Corfu, Mosul, and the Greek-Bulgarian clash of 1925—but these were dangerous crises at the time. No constructive friend of the League could claim that the Council had acted always with wisdom, dispatch, and complete success in dealing with them, though all this was true of the Greek-Bulgarian affair, which was still fresh in all minds at Geneva.

In any event the burden of doing something rested on the Council. Nearly every dispute that arose was complicated and difficult to deal with. Only after struggling with it for some time was it apparent whether an advisory opinion of the World Court would be useful in promoting a solution, or perhaps the only line of approach left. At such a point no outside body, like the United States Government, could act on a basis of perfect equality, especially since it would be without responsibility in the emergency. Of course the American executive would be very slow to veto the asking of advisory opinions, but in those years the Senate was the ultimate power in Washington and its machinery was dominated by the bitter-enders, who lost no opportunity to see something sinister whenever the League moved. How was the Council to know whether these men could be induced to keep silent or whether they would demand a veto? The United States did not need to have an interest in a case; it only needed to claim one, and the iron men on the Senate Committee on Foreign Relations were the ones to decide whether a claim should be made. Nothing was more established, either, than their habit of finding vague, remote, hypothetical dangers lurking behind each and every attempt at international action.

It was not therefore an easy thing for the members of the Court to agree that the United States Senate had now put itself on a basis of perfect equality with the League Council. It was more likely to appear that the Senate had established itself on a censorious pedestal above the seats of the Council members.

Must Action Be Unanimous in Requesting an Advisory Opinion? Again, should the League bind upon itself permanently the custom that an advisory opinion must be asked by a unanimous vote of the Council or the Assembly? It was quite probable that this would continue to be the practice, but the Covenant permitted questions of procedure to be decided by majority vote, and the argument for this view was strong. It was easy for the Senate to assume from its Olympian distance that the unanimity rule was fixed, but the recalcitrance of one or two governments might make it essential to ask for advisory opinions by a majority vote, if the League was to discharge its all-important function, in which case the American claim to a free veto would fall to the ground. Indeed, at the moment the Senate acted the most dangerous constitutional crisis in the life of the League was just boiling up.

When Germany was to be given a permanent seat on the Council, in accord with the Locarno agreements, Poland, Spain, and Brazil also set up claims for permanent seats, and Brazil went to the length of blocking action on Germany's admission, in March 1926, and of resigning from the League when the claim asserted by her dictator was denied. This crisis caused by the unanimity rule, which shook the League to its foundations, hardly provided the setting for an unconditional acceptance of the Senate's equality formula.

A Conference of Signatory States Called. On March 18, 1926, at the close of its grueling and depressing failure to bring Germany into the League, and the Locarno treaties into operation, the Council took up the Senate's demand to exercise irresponsibly a privilege of Council membership. Sir Austen Chamberlain suggested that the Court protocol, ratified by all Court members, could hardly be modified by a mere exchange of notes. The meaning of the fifth reservation was also not clear. It could be interpreted in a way that would hamper the work of the Council. This was not to be assumed, but the correct interpretation should be the subject of discussion and agreement. A conference between the United States and the nations belonging to the Court was accordingly called, to meet in Geneva, September 1, 1926.[1]

It is difficult to imagine a more reasonable or inevitable move, yet it was received in Washington with feigned amazement. The irreconcilables rejoiced, and condemned the Council strongly. Senator Borah proclaimed that the United

States would have to go through with it and "sit with" the League.[2] Here was something that could be represented as a dangerous political entanglement. President Coolidge declared repeatedly that he was opposed to sending any representative to the conference.[3]

Negotiation Refused. The State Department was thrown into a quandary by the invitation to the conference. It had not proposed the troublesome reservation, but it dared not negotiate for the Senate. That body had just expressed its ultimate wisdom. Nobody could modify that. Moreover, the United States, not being a signatory of the Court protocol, would have an uncertain standing in the conference. So Secretary Kellogg replied to the Council, in part:

I do not feel that any useful purpose could be served by the designation of a delegate by my government to attend a conference for this purpose. These reservations are plain and unequivocal and according to their terms they must be accepted by an exchange of notes between the United States and each of the forty-eight states signatory to the statute of the Permanent Court before the United States can become a party and sign the protocol. The resolution specifically provided this mode of procedure.

I have no authority to vary this mode of procedure or to modify the conditions and reservations or to interpret them, and I see no difficulty in the way of securing the assent of each signatory by direct exchange of notes, as provided by the Senate. It would seem to me to be a matter of regret if the Council of the League should do anything to create the impression that there are substantial difficulties in the way of such direct communication. This government does not consider that any new agreement is necessary to give effect to the conditions and reservations on which the United States is prepared to adhere to the Permanent Court. The acceptance of the reservations by all the nations signatory to the statute of the Permanent Court constitutes such an agreement.[4]

These paragraphs probably record the high point of the Senate's confidence that upon this planet its word is fiat.

The Senate had spoken, and it had, of course, said the last word. Its reservations, including the far-ramifying fifth proviso, were "plain and unequivocal"! All that the powers had to do was to accept them as written, and the Senate had told them plainly just how to do that. It was to be done in notes from "each of the forty-eight states signatory to the statute of the Permanent Court." Was this not clear? "The resolution specifically provided this mode of procedure." It said nothing about conference or discussion.

"I have no authority," said Secretary Kellogg, most truthfully, "to vary this mode of procedure or to modify the conditions and reservations or to interpret them." All that the forty-eight governments needed to do was to sign on the dotted line. There was "no difficulty" about that and it was "a matter of regret" that the Council should suggest anything to the contrary. No "new agreement" was necessary. Just a simple "acceptance of the reservations by all the nations signatory."

The Illusion That Our Wishes Were Fiat Throughout the Globe. It would be difficult for anyone to sit down and imagine a more presumptuous statement made by one government to many. It is clear also that Secretary Kellogg not only spoke for the Senate but for the executive. We had already assumed the status of a power equal and co-ordinate to the whole League of Nations—the assumption which was to nullify largely our efforts to work with the League when Japan began the Second World War in our own back yard, on September 21, 1931. In 1926 the afterglow of our military achievement in World War I convinced us that our wishes on any subject would naturally be accepted.

The Kellogg note to the Council also shows that the inconclusive end of the League fight in the Senate had obscured to us our actual importance to the other nations. We had not thought through the business of getting the acceptance of scores of nations to the concentrated suspicions emanating from the Senate. Almost everyone assumed that the Lodge reservations, or any others we cared to make, would be snapped up by the other peoples in their eagerness "to get us in." Had not Viscount Grey urged that the Lodge reservations be accepted, after spending four months in Washington at the end of the League controversy? And wasn't our co-operation so essential that we could name our own terms for it? We made these assumptions without calculating whether every foreign office in Latin America would accept our Monroe Doctrine reservation. Our good neighbors flocked into the League partly because of the uproar in this country about our high sovereignty in the New World. In accepting the League Covenant the Chilean government had specifically reserved the right to pass upon such amendments or modifications as might be made by states which had not ratified.

Few had stopped to think, before 1926, that our Shantung and Irish reservations had affronted powerful nationalistic sentiments abroad, or that the "one vote for the British Empire or six for us" demand was a deep offense to the best friends we had on earth. The British dominions could not possibly have let that one pass, without at least a long process of discussion and conference. On February 16, 1920, the Foreign Minister of Canada had given notice that, if this reservation were accepted by the other members of the League, Canada would resign.

It is true that in November 1919 Lodge thought that it would be sufficient to gain the consent of "three of the four principal Allied and Associated Powers, to wit, Great Britain, France, Italy, and Japan." In March 1920 this was amended to provide for approval by all four of the Allies, thus leaving the rights of the other twenty-eight signatories of the Covenant to one side, but by 1926 it was admitted that this would not do, that the express assent of each one of the forty-eight members of the Court was essential.

In retrospect one wonders that so many senators could have assumed that the required unanimous consent would be forthcoming. Slight reflection would tell them that it would be futile to send a list of captious points to forty-eight individuals, about something which concerned all of them, and expect unanimous acceptance by return mail. Anyone could foresee that every kind of reply would be received and that there would be no replies whatever from some. Why should it have been expected that the response would be different from dozens of governments, either in 1920 or in 1926?

How Far the Senate's Writ Ran. After 1926 the Senate was to learn that it had actually taken a thousand-to-one shot. By the end of 1927 five states had accepted the Senate's terms in toto, just as everybody was supposed to do, though two of these later withdrew their acceptance in part. The five which said yes were Cuba, Greece, Liberia, Albania, and Luxembourg. Six more important states did not reply at all. They were: Brazil, Bulgaria, Canada, Chile, Hungary, and New Zealand. Sixteen governments simply sent polite notes acknowledging receipt of the Senate's terms, without saying what they thought of them.[5] This, too, was altogether to be expected. Yet the Senate's highly perfected reservations required the simple, unconditional assent of the entire forty-eight governments. No reservations to reservations. No counterassertion of rights, fears, and susceptibilities; just simple acceptance by all.

Obviously a conference of the interested states offered the only conceivable chance that our highly suspicious approach toward the Court could be made effective. The League Council was doing the Senate a favor in assembling the representatives of twenty-two signatory states in Geneva, September 1926. The delegates deliberated in a careful and conciliatory manner for three weeks, and without any help from us, before embodying their conclusions in a Final Act, on September 23.

The Conference Friendly. The report to the Conference of its Committee of Eleven was as conciliatory as could have been desired. Its introductory paragraphs said:

It was the unanimous wish of the Conference to accept the offer by satisfying the United States' reservations as far as possible. The very creation of a Permanent Court of International Justice constitutes in itself and irrespective of the existence of the League of Nations so great a progress in the development of peaceful relations between States that every effort should be made to render that act fruitful of still further results.

The greater the number of states which have acceded to the Court the greater will be the Court's authority. It is to the interest of the States which founded the Court that all the other States of the world should agree to become parties thereto, even if they feel unable to become Members of the League of Nations. In particular, the possibility of the accession of the United States of America, as a State mentioned in the Covenant of the League of Nations, was provided for in the Protocol of signature of the Statute of the Court. It therefore seems quite natural that the States signatories of the Protocol, in presence of a proposal—even a conditional proposal—by the United States of America to accede to the Court, should adopt a favourable attitude.

On the other hand, the conditional character of the proposal is sufficiently explained by the fact that the United States of America is not a member of the League of Nations and does not desire to change its attitude. This fact must be taken into account and an endeavor must be made to reconcile the working of the Covenant with the important object of increasing the number of States which have acceded to the Court and with the requirement of the position of the United States.

The first three reservations were accepted outright and the fourth would have been accepted as Secretary Hughes had proposed it—that is, to provide that the Court's statute should not be amended without our consent. The Senate, however, had amended this reservation to give us the right of withdrawal. This, too, was accepted, but with the following counterreservation:

In order to assure equality of treatment, it seems natural that the signatory states, acting together and by not less than a majority of two thirds, should possess the corresponding right to withdraw their acceptance of the special conditions attached by the United States to its adherence to the said Protocol in the second part of the fourth reservation and in the fifth reservation. In this way the *status quo ante* could be re-established if it were found that the arrangement agreed upon was not yielding satisfactory results.

It is hoped, nevertheless, that no such withdrawal will be made without an attempt by a previous exchange of views to solve any difficulties which may arise.

A Counterreservation on Withdrawal Proposed. The logic of this position was irrefutable. If the United States was afraid that her sister nations would gang up on her, a free and unimpeded exit must be accorded to her. But if the suspicions and animosities so freely voiced in the Senate should hamper unduly the advisory-opinion function, the other members of the Court should have the right to decide, by not less than a two-thirds majority, to do without the collaboration of the United States.

For once the Senate was paid back in its own coin, in a manner to which no senator could object. If the Senate insisted on being forever suspicious of other peoples it could not complain if they returned the compliment. Nor was it merely a matter of reciprocating in kind. There was no prospect that the Senate would ever stop impugning other people's motives until somebody called a halt. Only hard experience could teach the intractables and perfectionists of the Senate that the world's business could not be transacted, or its peace be preserved, on the basis of trusting nobody. The shock of learning that reservations could be made to reservations was severe, but it was salutary. After the Senate's resounding "success" in demolishing the League of Nations, insofar as its power reached, the feeling had grown, in the Senate and out, that the Senate had the whip hand, and that its reach was long. It was as near lèse majesté as one could come to suggest that the veto power of the United States Senate was after all limited by the existence of some sixty other sovereignties, none of which regarded the Senate as the supreme fount of wisdom for the earth. Only hard contact with other sovereign wills could teach the Senate its limitations, a process which even now may be only begun.

To reconcile the Senate's claim to a free veto over advisory opinions, the September Conference took up the two parts of Reservation 5 separately. In reply to the first part, requiring public procedure for advisory opinions, it cited the current rules and agreed to consider their incorporation into a more permanent protocol.

Different Opinions on the Unanimity Issue. Concerning the second part of the fifth reservation demanding a veto on the giving of all advisory opinions, the Conference listened to speakers who had read the Senate debates, in the absence of an American spokesman, and agreed that the United States should be assured a position of equality with states represented on the Council or Assembly. But the Final Act denied that the presumption of action by unanimous vote in those bodies was established.

This conclusion was questioned even by pro-Court senators. It appeared to be taken for granted, they said, until our reservation was made. This was apparently true, yet the very raising of the point was sure to bring out differences of opinion. The Assembly had not exercised its right to ask for advisory opinions, but it might wish to do so, in which case a requirement of unanimity was likely to be impractical. The many small states in the Court and the League could not look with favor on a decision that they could never ask for an advisory opinion by a majority vote. There might be occasions when they would feel that the rights of one of their number urgently needed clarification, perhaps when threatened by a Great Power.

On the legal side, also, the experts differed. Dr. van Eysinga, the president of the September Conference, held that a request for an advisory opinion was a matter of substance, requiring unanimity, but M. Rolin, of Belgium, agreed with Sir Cecil Hurst, of Great Britain, that it might sometimes be a matter of substance and at others a matter of procedure, requiring only a majority vote. This was denied by the leading French jurist, M. Fromageot, who believed it must be one or the other. Others were in doubt, but opposed the forcing of an early decision on a matter of such great importance.[6]

Agreement Asked on the Exercise of Our Veto. Calling attention to the great importance which the members of the League attached to advisory opinions, and the intimate knowledge they would have in situations calling for them, the Conference felt that:

A State which is exempt from the obligations and responsibilities of the Covenant would occupy a different position. It is for this reason that the procedure to be followed by a non-member State in connection with requests for advisory opinions is a matter of importance and in consequence it is desirable that the manner in which the consent provided for in the second part of the fifth reservation will be given should form the object of a supplementary agreement which would ensure that the peaceful settlement of future differences between members of the League of Nations would not be made more difficult.[7]

The members of the Conference could not know how the veto asked by the United States would be applied. Would our Minister to Switzerland exercise the power, or the executive in Washington, or the Senate? And if the Senate was not in session, what then? These questions and others could be answered only by negotiation with the United States. This was proposed, as follows:

The manner in which the consent provided for in the second part of the fifth reservation is to be given, will be the subject of an understanding to be reached by the Government of the United States with the Council of the League of Nations.

The State signatories of the Protocol of December 16th, 1920, will be informed as soon as the understanding contemplated by the preceding paragraph has been reached.

Should the United States offer objection to an advisory opinion being given by the Court, at the request of the Council or the Assembly, concerning a dispute to which the United States is not a party or concerning a question other than a dispute between States, the Court will attribute to such objection the same force and effect as attaches to a vote against asking for the opinion given by a Member of the League of Nations either in the Assembly or in the Council.

The Conference thus accepted the fifth reservation in principle, but asked for the making of a working agreement. Senators were shocked because their conditional offer had been accepted conditionally. It had not occurred to them that others could play at that game. Yet the Conference had been more conciliatory than might have been expected. In adjourning, its president frankly said that he did not know what attitude the United States would take. "We have built a bridge," he said. "Let us hope America will cross it. Our constitutional difficulties in drafting this reply certainly have been greater than was dreamed of in the United States when the reservations were formulated.

We look to the United States to resume her place in the pacific settlement of international conflicts."[8]

The United States, however, did not reciprocate. Politely but firmly twenty-one governments had stood up to the United States Senate, an event in our national history so unique and unexpected that even the Administration was offended and nonplused. The action of the September Conference, forwarded to us twenty-one times from as many capital cities, as the niceties of our splendid isolation demanded, went unanswered.

Washington Offended. Finally, on November 12, 1926, the newspapers carried streamer heads saying "World Court Entry Only on Our Own Terms." This caption correctly summarized President Coolidge's Armistice Day speech. Taking a lofty view, he advised against any spirit of distrust or hatred toward other nations, remarking acidly that "the Old World had for generations indulged itself in that form of luxury."

Denying that we had profited by the war, he thought our reported unpopularity in Europe exaggerated, but explained it as follows: "We are a creditor nation. We are more prosperous than some others. This means that our interests have come within the European circle where distrust and suspicion, if nothing more, have been altogether too common. To turn such attention to us indicates at least that we are not ignored." Yet we should not fail to appreciate their trials and sufferings and extend to them "our patience, our sympathy, and such help as we believe will enable them to be restored to a sound and prosperous condition."

Then, after a strong statement pointing out the necessity of institutions in securing justice and the misrepresentation to which the World Court had been subjected, he came to this final paragraph but one: "While the nations involved cannot yet be said to have made a final determination, and from most of them no answer has been received, many have indicated that they are unwilling to concur in the conditions adopted by the resolution of the Senate. While no final determination can be made by our government until final answers are received, the situation has been sufficiently developed so that I feel warranted in saying that I do not intend to ask the Senate to modify its position. I do not believe the Senate would take favorable action on any such proposal, and unless the requirements of the Senate resolution are met by the other interested nations I can see no prospect of this country adhering to the Court."[9]

In this fashion ended, apparently, our second great effort to substitute world government for world war. An almost unanimous public sentiment had at length driven the Senate, inch by inch, to take the smallest possible step toward providing alternatives to war. The step was taken in a highly suspicious, conditional manner, and when the other nations concerned ventured to invite discussion of one reservation only, with a view to mutual agreement, we drew ourselves up haughtily and refused to negotiate. It was that or nothing. Take it or leave it!

Only seven years earlier the United States had stood upon a high level of world leadership never before attained by any nation. The people of every land looked to us confidently for leadership and for vision, for farseeing planning and execution in world organization. But seven years after 1919 we had plummeted down so far that the best the President of the United States could say was, "at least we are not ignored"!

CHAPTER VI

The Second Root Mission

LIKE THE LEAGUE, the Court now appeared to be dead, as far as the United States was concerned. Yet the Senate was not quite ready to cut completely the last avenue into the postwar community of nations. The current illusions of powerful isolation did not hide from some senators the implications of a total refusal on our part to place any confidence in the rest of humanity, including the sources of our own civilization. Until they read the Final Act of the September Conference other senators had not begun to understand the inevitable effect upon the rest of the world of our effort to make ourselves supersafe from it. Senator Trammell of Florida proposed, on February 7, 1927, that the Senate rescind its resolution of adherence to the Court, but this was rejected by a vote of 59 to 10.

Reconsideration Urged. By that time public opinion was fatigued and disappointed. At the close of the year, however, a nationwide petition was presented to President Coolidge urging a renewal of negotiations with the World Court signatories. This petition led the Scripps-Howard newspapers to urge this action upon the President. After recalling that he had said in his inaugural address: "We ought not to barter away our independence or our sovereignty, but we ought to engage in no refinements of logic, no sophistries, and no subterfuges, to argue away the undoubted duty of this country, by reason of the might of its numbers, the power of its resources and its position of leadership in the world, actively and comprehensively to signify its approval and to bear its full share of the responsibility of a candid and disinterested attempt at the establishment of a tribunal for the administration of even-handed justice between nation and nation," the Scripps-Howard editorial concluded:

In no state paper does the logic of President Coolidge appear to better advantage than in this. And it is to be hoped, as the petition of Monday suggests, that the President will indicate his willingness to continue along the same line. The Senate, in framing the conditions upon which the United States would adhere to the World Court, deliberately or otherwise threw the President's recommendations to the winds and indulged in so many refinements of logic, sophistries, and subterfuges that we were finally finessed out of the Court.

These reservations were more sounding than sound, more superficial than fundamental, and one of the most useful acts the President could do before he leaves the White House, as he has expressed his intention of doing, would be to tell the Senate so.

Not long afterward, on February 6, 1928, Senator Gillett, Republican, of Massachusetts, introduced a resolution suggesting to the President the advisability of a further exchange of views with the states signatory to the Court. In a statement on March 11 Gillett recalled that the September Conference had sent courteous expressions of hope that differences might be discussed and accommodated. Doubtless the Secretary of State had felt himself unable to answer for the Senate and had "prudently answered nothing," but so momentous a matter should not be allowed to die from inaction. He hoped that there might be some modification or clarification of the Senate resolution of adherence which would enable the President to take up the question with the powers again.[1]

The Gillett proposal evoked strong expressions of approval.

On February 12 the Portland *Oregonian,* one of the leading Republican papers of the West, noted a widespread demand for reconsideration. Senate reservations resembled an ultimatum, leaving no opening for further negotiation. Their "take it or leave it" form naturally inspired other people to leave them. Yet in the recent case the other nations had accepted some and "left the one regarding advisory opinions in such a shape that by negotiation we could gain all that we could reasonably ask." There was again "a studied effort to suppress discussion of this subject." But in the period after 1923 overwhelming public opinion had forced the Senate to yield, "even against the will of influential members who are determined enemies of the Court. The Gillett resolution gives opportunity for another such expression of public opinion and for another exertion of pressure on stubborn senators who cherish the delusion of American isolation."

The Gillett resolution was considered by the Committee on Foreign Relations at its usual glacial pace. The anti-Court members charged that it would give the Secretary of State authority to interpret the fifth reservation. Borah argued that the matter should be debated all over again. Finally after several sessions action was postponed on May 23, 1928, to its first meeting in December, by a vote of 9 to 8.

Negotiations Reopened. Shortly before this meeting was to be held President Coolidge expressed a willingness to renew negotiations, and on February 20, 1929, Secretary Kellogg made public a cordial note just sent to each of the World Court signatories. In it he frankly acknowledged that he had received five acceptances to the Senate's reservations, out of forty-eight. Our government desired to avoid any proposal which would interfere with or embarrass the work of the Council, "doubtless often perplexing and difficult, and it would be glad if it could dispose of the subject by a simple acceptance of the suggestions embodied in the final act and draft protocol adopted at Geneva on September 23, 1926."

There were, however, some elements of uncertainty still to be cleared up and since the 22 governments had shown appreciation of the reasons which had led to the adoption of Reservation 5, our government felt that the informal exchange of views which had been invited should "lead to agreement upon some provision which in unobjectionable form would protect the rights and interests of the United States as an adherent of the Court statute, and this expectation is strongly supported by the fact that there seems to be but little difference regarding the substance of these rights and interests."[2]

This friendly agreement to negotiate did not come too soon, since there was a movement among the smaller states in the League to obtain a decision that advisory opinions could be requested by a majority vote. On September 8, 1928, M. Motta, of Switzerland, had asked the Council to decide the point and a similar move was made in the Assembly. Should either body declare in favor of the majority-vote viewpoint, the possibility of our obtaining a veto on advisory opinions would be gone.

There had also been a positive development which suggested that the closed issue of the Court should be reopened. On the same day that M. Motta made his proposal the Assembly elected Charles E. Hughes to fill the vacancy on the World Court bench created by the resignation of Judge John Bassett Moore. Mr. Hughes received the votes of forty-one out of forty-eight states in the Assembly and a unanimous ballot in the Council. He promptly telegraphed that he felt honored by the election and would feel it a privilege to serve. It was evident that though the other nations were not ready to approve unconditionally all the Senate's super-safeguards against association with them, they were quite ready to have the most eminent American lawyer enter the World Court and see for himself whether it was as danger-ous as it had been represented. Furthermore, the Assembly provided for a committee of jurists to consider changes in the statute of the Court, ostensibly in view of the approach-ing general election of judges, but also perchance to bind on the Court some of the good rules that the Americans were so nervous about. At least an opportunity to appease our fears was opened.

These developments gave the intellectual leaders of the Republican party another opportunity to try to extricate us from the pit of impotent futility in which we found our-selves. A student who has recently studied the period closely found repeated evidences of frustration in the minds of the people. "In America," he says, "as we read the letters and newspapers and public speeches of the period, one gets the feeling of a kind of guilt complex. People felt, so to speak, that Uncle Sam had hardly played the part of a sportsman in suddenly backing out of the game after forcing upon it a new set of rules."[3] No one who lived through these years needs to be told how poignant the sense of frustration was. It was true that the senators who blocked any effort to win the peace and defend it were acting within their constitutional rights, but that did not hide the fact that a deep moral offense was being committed against the other nations, against our soldier dead, and against the future peace.

It must have been particularly galling to men like Hughes and Root to have even the juridical approach to world order completely blocked, as far as we were concerned. They were the fathers of that line of development. They had built it in our own tradition. To Root, especially, it had been a lifelong endeavor. He therefore accepted, at the age of eighty-five, an invitation to go to Europe again to sit on the new Commission and exercise once more his incomparable talent for finding formulas which seemed to provide common cover for the most antagonistic views.

Sailing to Europe in midwinter, on February 15, 1929, Root took with him all the support the executive could offer. He had helped Secretary Kellogg draft the friendly note to the members of the Court which was released on the twentieth, as Root neared Europe. Immediately after his election as a judge of the World Court, Hughes had taken a prominent part in the successful campaign to elect Herbert Hoover to the presidency, and in his inaugural address, March 4, Hoover gave strong support to another approach to the Court. Stressing how the Court was peculiarly identified with American ideals and statesmanship, he explained that the reservations sought no special privilege for us but only clarification of our relation to advisory opinions. The way should be found "by which we may take our proper place in a movement so fundamental to the progress of peace."

Root had taken care to talk with Senate leaders before he left and in Geneva he began at once to explain individually to members of the Council the formula which he hoped would solve the difficulty. Soon, on March 9, the Council voted to authorize the Commission of jurists to take up the question of American adherence.

The Root Formula. Root's plan tried to solve the deadlock by reaffirming in full the Senate's claim to a veto over advisory opinions and by setting up rules to govern the exercise of the veto which would be likely to reduce its use to a minimum. The United States should be notified of each request for an advisory opinion, preferably before the request, and discussion invited. If finally discussion should disclose:

(1) that no agreement can be reached as to whether the question does touch an interest of the United States within the true meaning of the second paragraph of this article; and (2) that submission of the question is still insisted upon after attributing to the objection of the United States the same force and effect as attaches to a vote against asking for the opinion given by a member of the League of Nations either in Assembly or Council; and if it also appears that the United States has not been able to find the submission of the question so important for the general good as to call upon the United States to forego its objection, in that particular instance leaving the request to be acted upon by the Court without in any way binding the United States; then it shall be deemed that owing to material difference of view regarding the proper scope or practice of requesting advisory opinions, the arrangement now agreed upon is not yielding satisfactory results, and that exercise of powers of withdrawal provided in Article XII hereof will follow naturally without any imputation of unfriendliness or unwillingness to co-operate generally for peace and good will.[4]

In explaining the scheme to the Commission he frankly said that he didn't suppose this complicated machinery would ever come into use, but if it did he felt sure that agreement would result. He did not believe the apprehensions aroused in both Washington and Geneva to be well founded, but both had to be guarded against.[5]

The Root plan was somewhat simplified by Sir Cecil Hurst and adopted by the Commission on March 18. Its report stated that the Commission felt the advisory-opinion function too useful to abandon and it did not feel able to recommend that requests require unanimity. It was too soon to force a decision on this issue. All that could be done was to guarantee the United States a position of equality in this matter with members of the League and leave the question of unanimity to be settled "by the gradual evolution of recognized and obligatory practice."

The Root Plan Accepted by a Second International Conference. To surmount the immense difficulty of mobilizing the acceptance of forty-eight states, the Commission urged that the signatory states send delegates to the 1929 Assembly empowered to act on the proposed Protocol for the Accession of the United States. They did so and a Second Conference of Signatories was opened at Geneva on September 4, 1929. Being assured by the secretary-general of the League that the Secretary of State of the United States considered that the protocol would effectively meet the American reservations, the Conference unanimously accepted it, as did the Tenth Assembly. It was opened for signature on September 14, 1929, and promptly signed for many states. In succeeding years the governments ratified the protocol until, at the close of 1942, forty-two of the essential states had deposited ratifications in Geneva. Only Bolivia, Brazil, Chile, Haiti, Nicaragua, Paraguay, Peru, and El Salvador—all American states—had not done so.[6] Not a single government in the old world, the quarter toward which the Senate had directed its fears, had withheld its consent. Nor would any of the American states, presumably, if the United States had ratified the protocol.

Article 1 of the 1929 Protocol of Accession said: "The states signatories of the said protocol accept the special conditions attached by the United States in the five reservations mentioned above to its adherence to the said protocol upon the terms and conditions set out in the following articles." Articles 2 and 3 provided that we should have a full part in electing the judges and that the statute of the Court could not be amended without the consent of all contracting states. Article 4 met the first part of Reservation

5 by saying: "The Court shall render advisory opinions in public session after notice and opportunity for hearing substantially as provided in the now existing Articles 73 and 74 of the rules of the Court."

Article 5 dealt with the Senate's main objection as follows:

With a view to insuring that the Court shall not without the consent of the United States entertain any request for an advisory opinion touching any dispute or question in which the United States has or claims an interest, the Secretary-General of the League of Nations shall, through any channel designated for that purpose by the United States, inform the United States of any proposal before the Council or Assembly of the League for obtaining an advisory opinion from the Court and thereupon, if desired, an exchange of views shall proceed with all convenient speed between the Council or the Assembly of the League and the United States.

Whenever a request for an advisory opinion comes to the Court the Registrar shall notify the United States thereof, among the other States mentioned in the now existing Article 73 of the rules of the Court, stating a reasonable time limit fixed by the President within which a written statement by the United States concerning the request will be received. If for any reason no sufficient opportunity for an exchange of views upon such a request should have been afforded and the United States advises the Court that the question upon which the opinion of the Court is asked is one that affects the interests of the United States, the proceedings shall be stayed for a period sufficient to enable such an exchange of views between the Council or the Assembly and the United States to take place.

With regard to requesting the advisory opinion of the Court in any case covered by the preceding paragraphs, there shall be attributed to an objection of the United States the same force and effect as is attached to a vote against asking for an opinion given by a member of the League of Nations in the Council or in the Assembly.

If after the exchange of views provided for in paragraphs one and two of this article it shall appear that no agreement can be reached and the United States is not prepared to forego its objection, the exercise of powers of withdrawal provided for in Article 8, hereof, will follow naturally without any imputation of unfriendliness or unwillingness to co-operate generally for peace and good will.[7]

Article 6 gave to the protocol the same force and effect as the statute of the Court and bound any future signatory of the protocol of December 16, 1920, to accept its provisions.

Article 7 provided that all signatories of the 1920 protocol and the United States must ratify, and Article 8 preserved the right of the contracting states to withdraw their acceptance, as follows:

On their part, each of the other Contracting States may at any time notify the Secretary-General of the League of Nations that it desires to withdraw its acceptance of the special conditions attached by the United States to its adherence to the Protocol of December 16, 1920. The Secretary-General shall immediately give communication of this notification to each of the States signatories of the present Protocol. The present Protocol shall be considered as ceasing to be in force if and when, within one year from the date of receipt of the said notification, not less than two thirds of the Contracting States other than the United States shall have notified the Secretary-General of the League of Nations that they desire to withdraw the above-mentioned acceptance.

The one-year time limit laid down was so short as to make it practically impossible for thirty-three or more states to signify their dissatisfaction with our conduct concerning the Court, unless friction was very acute.[8]

Once again the nations had gathered to consider what to do about that young Samson among them whose senatorial guardians feared he might lose his locks in some unguarded moment. This time surely they had assuaged the fears that Sam could not safely appear even in a court of law manned by his mother nations, by his friendly young cousins from the British dominions, by his really mature friends, the Scandinavians, Dutch, and Swiss, and by his Latin brothers from the New World.

But by the time the World Court protocols had been signed the era of carefree isolation, untrammeled by any political entanglements or responsibility, had exploded in Wall Street, prostrating the giant of the Western world. Assured by the Senate that no responsibility rested upon them, moral or actual, that they need only "eat, drink, and be merry," the American people had gambled in everything from the sands of Florida to their very existence in an anarchical world. And when the great boom suddenly burst, in October 1929, destroying the funds from all over the world which had been sucked into the American vortex, and drying up instantly the prodigal American loans upon which a false world prosperity had been built, there was little time to think about world courts.

A year later, in December 1930, there was apprehension among the Republican leaders that the submission of the World Court protocols to the Senate might block emergency legislation in the short session and precipitate an extra session. President Hoover nevertheless laid them before the Senate on December 10, and as the Senate clerk finished reading his message Senator Borah rose and put into the *Congressional Record* an editorial from the New York *Evening Sun*, entitled, "When the League Court Comes Out, Kill It!"

Oppugnation in the Senate Not Allayed. One could not say that this defiance was amazing, because it was so usual, but it did illuminate the chronic state of war waged in the Senate against the President's conduct of our foreign policy.

George H. Haynes, the leading authority on the Senate, says of this incident:

That single page in the *Congressional Record* presents with startling clarity a chronic "oppugnation" and obstructionism in the Senate's dealing with foreign relations such as could not last a week in any other nation's parliament in its relation with the "Foreign Office." The President of the United States urges that a policy, long considered and clearly endorsed by his party, be carried into effect by the Senate nominally controlled by that party. Instantly the chairman of the Committee on Foreign Relations— "a second Secretary of State," as Lord Bryce characterized the holder of that chairmanship—virtually announced to the world that his utmost endeavor shall be exerted to defeat that purpose.[9]

In the Foreign Relations Committee a vote was promptly taken, 10 to 9, to postpone consideration for another year, in fear of the extra session, though a hearing was held on January 21, 1931, at which Elihu Root spoke for the Protocol of Adherence and submitted a carefully reasoned memorandum, ten pages long, in which he sought to show that the Senate's fears and demands had been fully met.

The eminent Republican elder statesman had courageously done what he could, but his word had no more effect upon the Senate than had the pleas of three Presidents and as many Secretaries of State. Always there were men on the Committee on Foreign Relations whose fear of the impending dangers could not be allayed, though unfortunately they were blind to the real and terrible dangers into which we were drifting while their hands paralyzed the helm of the ship of state. While they insisted that the danger of political sandbagging by the World Court must be totally guarded against, the sands of time had run out. The Second World War was about to begin on the plains of Manchuria.

The precious decade during which the peace might have been consolidated had been frittered away, so far as the world's greatest nation was concerned, by the die-hards always entrenched on the Committee. The original dozen bitter-enders had grimly called themselves the "Battalion of Death." Little did they and their successors know how much death they were inviting.

CHAPTER VII

Further Years of Delay

A FEW MONTHS AFTER Mr. Root had placed the World Court problem again in the lap of the Senate the Court handed down an advisory opinion which gave its American opponents an opportunity to proclaim triumphantly that it had proved itself to be a "political" court.

The Austro-German Customs Union Opinion. In the spring of 1931 the world prosperity based on reckless American lending was rapidly drying up, following the collapse of the American boom in October 1929. To mitigate the effects of the spreading economic paralysis, and also to give the German Republic something with which to combat the consequent upsurge of Hitlerism, the German and Austrian governments signed, on March 19, 1931, an agreement for a limited customs union between them.

They were greatly handicapped in framing the treaty by the existence of two recent treaties which had sought to prevent just such a contingency. Article 88 of the peace treaty of St.-Germain, September 10, 1919, provided: "The independence of Austria is inalienable otherwise than with the consent of the Council of the League of Nations. Consequently, Austria undertakes in the absence of the consent of the said Council to abstain from any act which might directly or indirectly or by any means whatever compromise her independence, particularly, and until her admission to membership of the League of Nations, by participation in the affairs of another power."

Later also, when the League of Nations was working out the financial reconstruction of Austria, she was required to agree again, in a protocol of October 4, 1922, that she would "abstain from any negotiations or from any economic or financial engagement calculated directly or indirectly to compromise that independence." It was specified further that this did not prevent Austria from maintaining "her freedom in the matter of customs tariffs and commercial or financial agreements, and, in general, in all matters relating to her economic regime or her commercial relations, provided always that she shall not violate her economic independence by granting to any state a special regime or exclusive advantages calculated to threaten this independence."

The signature of the 1931 agreement for an Austro-German customs union threw Europe instantly into political uproar. France and her allies remembered how the *Zollverein* had preceded the formation of the German Empire and assumed that another customs union was the first step toward the forbidden *Anschluss* between Germany and Austria. Germany's position was so weak, both financially and legally, that she was obliged to consent that the World Court pass upon the apparent infringement of two treaties. No one could deny that the interpretation of disputed treaties is the prime function of international judicial tribunals and a clearer need for interpretation had never existed. If ever there was a case for judicial determination this was it. Never, either, had the wisdom of establishing the advisory-opinion function been so clearly demonstrated. The League Council was not fitted to act as a court, yet if treaties were to have any continuing validity, something had to be done. Of course the issue was primarily political, said Manley Hudson, but it had legal aspects which conditioned any political solution.[1]

The Court held oral hearings in the case, July 20 to August 5, and handed down a closely divided decision on September 5, 1931, in which eight judges held that the proposed customs union violated the First Geneva Protocol. One of the eight was not willing to say that the Treaty of St.-Germain was also violated. Seven judges denied that either treaty was transgressed. They insisted that "the Court is not concerned with political considerations nor with political consequences." The agreement between Germany and Austria had been concluded on a basis of complete equality; it provided for "assimilation" of the customs regimes, not their "fusion"; it assumed the continued independence of Austria and did not presently threaten her independence. Beyond that the Court was not justified in going.

Political Bias Alleged. This minority opinion was manna to the American objectors. Here were seven good men and true, most upright judges, who had been overruled by eight bad men, scheming political judges. Was not the danger of venturing into this nest of intrigue now finally proved? The nationality of the judges was quickly scrutinized and it was noted that the minority had in it judges of American, British, Dutch, and German origin. Here was a good Nordic bloc, and (sure enough!) the majority contained six judges of French, Spanish, Italian, and Latin-American origin—a Latin bloc of lesser breeds! The opposition looked again and saw that the good minority was derived from wise nations who were helping Germany to recover her feet, while the bad majority was led by men from nations which were trying to hold Germany down.

The objectors were so totally political and nationalistic in their thinking that they could not conceive of judges on a world court acting upon anything but political bias, if politics was involved. The Court is "nothing but a political body," exulted Hiram Johnson,[2] and Edwin M. Borchard, of Yale University, quickly charged that "the Council of the League has thus used the Court and the Court has avowedly permitted itself to be used to achieve a political goal." The Court had presumed "to pass upon a political question on speculative forecasts of possible political consequences." This bad development was due to the new judges lately elected to the Court. They had now created "a danger which cannot be minimized." Moreover, concluded Borchard urbanely, "To a person interested in European welfare, the very fact that the legality or propriety of such a customs arrangement could be placed in issue is a symbol of European political conditions." Apparently there had been no judicial fact to be determined and the very suggestion that there was proved how bad and dangerous these "European political conditions" were.[3]

Replying to Borchard's further stricture that the exclusion of an Austrian *ad hoc* judge from the bench had been decisive, in view of the 8–7 decision, Philip C. Jessup, of Columbia University, termed the charges of political alignment on the decision "incapable of proof." He pointed out that in the preliminary decision to deny Austria an *ad hoc* judge, five of the seven minority judges, including the German judge, had voted to exclude an Austrian judge, while the Italian, Spanish, and Polish judges, supposed to be so prejudiced against the customs union, had voted to admit him.*

American Journal of International Law (1932), Vol. 26, p. 107. The names and nationalities of the majority judges were as follows: Altamira (Spain), Bustamante (Cuba), Fromageot (France), Guerrero (Salvador), Negulesco (Rumania), Rostworowski (Poland), Urrutía (Colombia) and Anzilotti (Italy).

The seven dissenting judges were: Adatci (Japan), Van Eysinga (Netherlands), Hurst (England), Kellogg (United States), Rolin-Jaequemyns (Belgium), Schücking (Germany) and Wang (China).

The argument that it was all politics also left unexplained why the Belgian judge voted with the minority, or why the Chinese and Japanese judges did not disagree. It assumed further that the three Latin-American judges who did agree were all men lacking the judicial mind, an unlikely event. The ease with which a verdict can be said to be political or judicial, as one wishes, was brought out by Jessup's comment on Borchard's statement that "fifteen judges apparently agreed that the specific plan before them for consideration constituted no impairment of Austria's independence, but eight think it might eventually lead to such a result. Thus a great court . . . converts a legal question into a political question and decides it on considerations involving exclusively political speculation. . . ." This seems to convict the Court of "political" action, said Jessup, until it is recalled that both of the treaties before the Court for application forbade not only the actual impairment of Austria's independence, but any acts "which *might*, directly or *indirectly*," compromise her independence.[4]

When one looked at the treaty words italicized, then the verdict of the Court ascended from the malodorous swamps of political chicanery into the higher realms of unsullied judicial determination.

The Majority Opinion Sound. John W. Davis, one of the ablest and most conservative lawyers of his generation, maintained that the Court not only worked out the case juridically but correctly. He had "no difficulty whatever in concluding that both by its express terms and by its probable consequences" the proposed Austro-German customs regime would "compromise, endanger, imperil, and threaten —to use the words on which the majority and minority of the Court were agreed—that independence, that unfettered freedom of will and of decision, which, lacking the consent of the Council, Austria had solemnly covenanted to preserve inviolate." The distinction of the minority judges between "customs union" and "assimilation of tariff policies" was "a mere play on words." After studying all the opinions and the texts on which they were based, Davis not only found enough fully to justify the decision but "nothing whatever to warrant the conclusion that the eight judges in the majority were guided by political motives from which the seven in the minority were miraculously delivered."[5]

In all probability it was the minority of the Court which was most influenced by political motives. Being acutely aware of the deepening economic distress which afflicted Germany and Austria, and everybody else, and feeling that a customs union between these two German states would help both, they decided not to look too hard at the terms of the treaties.

There was certainly the most powerful contemporary compulsion to move the judges in that direction. While the case was before the Court the greatest Austrian bank, the *Kredit Anstalt* was found to be insolvent, on May 11, 1931, precipitating a world financial panic which prostrated Austria, then overwhelmed Germany, swept over the Channel to tumble England from the gold standard, and then returned to the United States, which had given it birth, to close every bank in the nation for the last rites of Normalcy. In the earlier stages of this catastrophe American and British investors were deeply troubled about the great volume of short-term loans which they had in Germany. In June 1931 President Hoover was moved even to suspend the precious war debts, so allegedly endangered by the existence of the World Court, and reparations, in an effort to save the private American funds in Germany and to halt the deluge where it was. But it could not be halted, and it had done its work so well by the time the Court handed down its verdict on the Austro-German customs union, September 5, that neither Germany nor Austria felt able to protest the decision.

The economic disaster which attended the case obscured the crucial political issues at stake. Isolationist Americans argued, openly or by implication, that the German-Austrian attempt to form a customs union was a normal and laudable effort of two good nations to better themselves economically. This argument seemed valid in financial circles and to some liberals who believed in self-determination. But the attempted customs union was actually a "sword thrust at the vital center" of the whole European structure established after the last war. Nothing could have indicated more clearly a new German hegemony of Europe. When Germany and Austria suddenly confronted Europe with the proposed customs union, on March 21, 1931, it was the voice of doom to Czechoslovakia and to Poland behind her. It was notice to everybody that the pivot of the whole European system was about to change hands, opening the way for a new *drang nach Osten* down through Central Europe and the Balkans. "Every informed European knew the meaning and peril of the move,"[6] but many Americans in their isolation were completely blind to its meaning and saw in it only two needy sovereignties trying to earn an honest penny.

Oblivious of the tremendous political dynamite which was scarcely concealed under the customs-union proposal, American opponents of the World Court used the Court's opinion to bolster considerably their slender case.

The Vital Consideration. In 1932 too many friends of the Court admitted by implication that it had probably erred. It was the easier to do so since ex-Secretary of State Kellogg, now a judge of the World Court in place of Charles E. Hughes, had voted in the minority, along with the British and Dutch judges. The Court's supporters did not always go on to insist, either, that the supremely vital thing is not infallibility in a court's judgments but the fact that it is there, to render sometimes imperfect judgments but to prevent the settlement of disputes by force.

The integrity of the World Court was certified in no uncertain terms by Charles E. Hughes, after his return from working as a judge on the World Court to head the United States Supreme Court. He explained in detail how each judge labors "in his own sanctum on his own opinion, knowing that it will be analyzed and eviscerated by equally if not more able men who have studied the case with the same attention." The judges desired the respect of their colleagues and hoped for the esteem of the world. The only way to get either was by unremitting industry and the candid expression of views. "That is what I have found characteristic of the international Court," said Hughes, adding that his work in it had been "one of the most interesting experiences of my life." Referring to the contention that we are so rich and powerful that we must be chary about any international body, he believed there was "a far greater degree of insecurity in the long run in such a highly objectionable and intransigent attitude."[7]

Root's Work Set Aside. However, such considerations did not clarify the Court question to the Senate Committee on Foreign Relations. The pressure of the domestic crisis prevented that body from taking up the three Court protocols until March 2, 1932. Then Senator David Reed promptly proposed acceptance of the protocols "with the clear understanding" that the Court "shall not, without the consent of the United States, entertain any request for an advisory opinion touching any dispute or question in which the United States has or claims an interest." The beloved words of this reservation were at once adopted unanimously by the Committee. Since they had been promulgated in 1926 these phrases had been the subject of two international conferences, the first of which pored over the *Congressional Record* to see what they might mean, with the conclusion that clarification was necessary. The second conference, in 1929, was convinced that Mr. Root's formula made the reservation acceptable. It said so plainly and Mr. Root had earnestly assured the Committee that this was true. The Protocol of Adhesion, he said, "established as law the second part of the fifth Senate reservation, without any change. . . . There are no terms or conditions attached to this acceptance which affect this prohibition or the rights of the United States under it."

But the unequivocal declaration of so great a lawyer as Mr. Root could not settle the matter for the lawyers of the Committee. Had not someone else said to the contrary? And had not the acceptance of the powers been embodied in a treaty of several articles and many words? Maybe there was a shade of meaning somewhere in these lines which would rise up sometime to trouble the Senate's immortal paragraph. The only thing to do was to start from scratch again and enunciate the fifth reservation as if nothing had happened. It did not matter that the powers had labored patiently over these lines again and again. That in itself was an offense. They had not returned a simple yes to the Senate's ultimatum, in forty-eight separate notes. That they must now do. There was no other way by which the matter could ever be closed.

Even Senator Thomas J. Walsh, friend of the Court, argued that the repromulgation of the fifth reservation was merely a declaration that we understood the new protocol to be an acceptance of the original Senate demands. The old maxim of the Senate, "if there is the faintest doubt, cover it by a reservation," was now stepped up into a new law: if there is any conceivable doubt about the acceptance of a reservation, reiterate it. It might seem to many nations that the Senate had not bothered to study the Protocol of Adhesion, but no matter.

All this was, of course, meat and drink to Borah. He maintained that the reiteration of Reservation 5 was more than a simple declaration of our own understanding. It was, he said, a reservation, requiring the approval of the signatory powers, and many of the strongest advocates of the Court agreed with him. Confusion was now gloriously compounded. To clear it all up Senator Pittman, by now an increasingly doubtful friend of the Court, offered on March 16 a proposed resolution by which the Senate asked President Hoover to ascertain if the signatory powers agreed that the fifth reservation was not affected by the protocol of 1929.[8] Since there was doubt in the Senate, the President should poll the forty-eight powers and see whether they meant what they said in this new protocol, and this should be done before the Senate moved further in its millennial approach to the Court.

This *démarche* naturally delighted the opponents of the Court, so much so that one of them, Senator James Hamilton Lewis of Illinois, who had completely backslid from his earlier pro-League position, blandly offered a motion to postpone further discussion in the Committee until the Geneva Disarmament Conference closed, when Senator Swanson, a delegate, could report the "actual and true feeling" of the other governments toward the United States.

Secretary Stimson's Assurances Rejected. No action was taken on any of these proposals. Deadlock was beautifully complete. To clear it up Secretary of State Stimson was summoned. He had been sent for earlier but, having a heavy cold, he had sent a letter to the Committee, on March 22, in which he endorsed Root's interpretation of the Protocol of Adhesion absolutely. He concurred that it "fully" accepted the fifth reservation and agreed with Root that it was a prohibition on the Court, not the Council or Assembly, a prohibition now incorporated into the Court's statute. The prohibition on the Court was absolute and "nowhere, either in Mr. Root's draft or in the final draft, is there any term or condition affecting it."

The Senate had not demanded any veto over the *requesting* of advisory opinions, said Stimson, but the other governments had now given us a certain amount of control even over the making of such requests. In the protocol of 1929 they were giving us a special protection, "one given to no other nation." The scores of other nations which had joined the Court had never requested or felt the need of such protection, "although nearly all of them are weaker and smaller than we are and thus presumptively more in need of such protection against being overreached by their fellows." By joining, concluded Stimson, "we incur absolutely no liabilities (except the insignificant liability to pay our share of the Court's expenses), while on the contrary we gain a power to exercise our influence not only in the choice of the judges of the Court but in its methods of procedure as well, which we do not now have."[9]

Did this forthright statement of evident truth clear the confused minds of the senators and convince them that their interminable teapot tempest had already brewed far too long? On the contrary, it made matters worse in the Committee. There was heated debate behind closed doors. Borah declared that the Secretary's letter was "unsatisfactory" and "led to confusion," and Pittman agreed that it was inconsistent with previous statements made by Stimson. Accordingly the Secretary of State had to appear and explain himself, but after a long discussion, on April 6, "the situation remained the same."[10]

Confusion Compounded. Naturally this delightful confusion spread to the Senate itself, convincing Democratic

Majority Leader Robinson that it would be wisest to keep the protocols in the Committee until the next session. But the controversy continued for another month. Senators who had fought on opposite sides of the question for years often found themselves comrades in arms. Pittman's resolution to require the governments to say that they had accepted the fifth reservation was defeated 11 to 8, on April 14, but unconvertible Senator Moses at once stepped into the breach with a reservation which required the powers to say yes again unequivocally, in forty-eight notes, but postponed this act of obeisance to the Senate from the instant present to the future. The powers were required to indicate "through an exchange of notes" (no conference, mind you!) their renewed acceptance of the fifth reservation "as a part and a condition of adherence by the United States to the said protocol."

This reservation having been adopted by one vote, the clock had been successfully turned back to the year 1. Yet two ancient rites remained to be performed. The inevitable words saying that our disputes could go before the Court only "through general or special treaties"—that is, by action of two thirds of the Senate—were added, along with the orthodox phrases of Hague Conference memory about our "not intruding upon, interfering with, or entangling in" political questions. No chance could be missed to force the powers to read this article of pure American faith.

In this form a resolution of adherence was voted out of committee on May 12, though only by a margin of 11 to 9, and submitted to the Senate on June 1, 1932, accompanied by a long report signed jointly by Thomas J. Walsh and Simeon D. Fess, in which they personally repudiated the Moses reservation and argued persuasively for a final end to the controversy. If there was any peril in the Court to us it was "shared by every signatory to the protocol. Moreover, we are even now in exactly that peril. . . . We could not escape the persuasive force of a decision by so respectable a court even though we held entirely aloof from it."[11]

To this basic truth, which reduced to such small proportions the whole hullabaloo about the Court, the two senators might have added that on the whole face of the globe there was only one center of obfuscation and obscurantism about the World Court, the Committee on Foreign Relations of the United States Senate.

Moses and Johnson were so encouraged by the way confusion bred confusion that they threatened to force action on the Committee report, feeling that they could defeat adherence to the Court. Borah, however, was not so confident. When asked when he thought it would come up in the Senate he replied, "So far as I am concerned, never." The majority of the Senate continued to be in favor of giving the Court a highly qualified nod of recognition, but its friends agreed that now was not the time.

The New York *Times* summarized the situation, on May 16, 1932, as follows: "Dickens' Circumlocution Office was a miracle of speed compared with the Foreign Relations Committee of the Senate when dealing with the World Court. Year after year, session of Congress after session of Congress, it goes on weaving a tangled web about the whole subject. Just now it has made a report to the Senate, but with so many reservations, with so many wire-drawn objections and scruples, that action upon the matter seems impossible."

The national conventions met soon thereafter and both endorsed the Court once more, the Republicans more strongly. Their platform commended this step toward the settlement of international disputes by the rule of law. We should join our influence and "gain a voice in this institution, which would offer us a safer, more judicial and expeditious instrument" than arbitration. The Democratic platform simply advocated "adherence to the World Court with the pending reservations."[12]

Party Platforms and Public Opinion Ignored. These declarations served to underline the fact that the party platforms had absolutely no effect upon many senators. On March 23 the nation's greatest leader of women, Mrs. Carrie Chapman Catt, had addressed a letter to Senator Borah in which she asked if the support of senators for party platforms was not to be expected. A few days later, on March 28, the Republican Women's World Court Committee, with leaders from many states, wrote to Borah that they believed the Protocol of Accession to be "an express acceptance of the Senate's fifth reservation" and that it left "unimpaired the power of veto over advisory opinions claimed by that reservation."

On December 12, 1932, two equally cogent letters were released by the American Foundation. One was addressed to the Republican members of the Senate, the other to the Democratic senators. Each was signed by about sixty outstanding citizens. The Democratic letter urged that the Senate's 1926 reservations had been completely fulfilled. The Republican statement reasoned that, "far from constituting a reason for again deferring action, the present troubled condition of the world points imperatively to the need for clear understanding of the stabilizing principle of judicial settlement of those disputes which will constantly arise between nations, the more frequently as their economic interrelations become the more complex." The Republicans urged that the delay be terminated and a vote reached before March 4, a result which was forestalled by the defeat of President Hoover for re-election and the blocking by the Democrats and insurgents of an executive session of the Senate during the short session, to prevent action on a list of Hoover's nominations for public offices.

The steadfast tide of informed opinion for the World Court was impressively demonstrated by the American Foundation on April 26. Leaders in all occupations to the number of 12,564 had been circularized, and 7,453 had responded in support of the Court. Only 302 replied in opposition and a still smaller number, 209, were noncommittal. But overwhelming expressions of support had no meaning to the opposition. When France defaulted on her war debt Senator David A. Reed of Pennsylvania declared, on December 16, 1932, "Now I trust that everybody will see that it will never do for us to enter the World Court." If the two things had any relation, commented the New York *Times* the next day, the French default would be an argument for using the Court, not avoiding it.

The Democrats Await a More Convenient Season. When the new Democratic Congress met in special session the majority leader, Senator Robinson, at once expressed the opinion that the World Court protocols should be reported from the Committee, to which they had automatically reverted. The Court proposal should be disposed of, he said on March 28, 1933; "It's been around here long enough." The Committee, however, postponed action for a week and "friends" of the Court began to express fear of prolonged debate that would halt the new Administration's domestic program. Robinson still urged action, but on April 5, after conference with President Roosevelt, he moved that the protocols stay in Committee. Their discussion in the Senate, said Arthur Krock in the New York *Times*, would present senators hostile to the Court "with an incomparable subject for timeless oratory." They could take the floor for a long speech during the debate on almost any bill. "Hundreds of thousands if not millions of words would certainly be uttered by resourceful and learned opponents."

The fear of the terrible dozen, now augmented by new

recruits, still lay upon all proposals for world co-operation. The wrath of the objectors could not be risked. Sheltered behind the Senate's extreme reluctance to curb debate, they could hold up everything. So while Hitler, newly come to power, turned all Germany into a roaring furnace of preparation for war the World Court was put to sleep again in the Senate's pigeonholes. All was still once more, except for a flash of penetrating reason from Major General John F. O'Ryan, on November 11, 1933—that melancholy anniversary of a wasted victory. On the day when it was difficult for anyone to forget the unredeemed national promises to prevent the recurrence of the colossal stupidities of the First World War, General O'Ryan declared that the only substitute for war is "one of law, international in scope, binding upon all units of world society, possessing not only a world court or courts to determine international disputes, but with full police power to enforce the judgments of the court."

So much was plainly required. But as both Hitler and Mussolini plunged to imitate Japan's example of successful conquest President Roosevelt's disposition to counter them by bolstering the institutions of international order did not increase. He was still in the early nationalistic period of the New Deal, when the isolationist bent of some of the early brain-trusters dictated full emphasis on economic recovery by our own efforts.

"*Not Opportune.*" Lame-duck Congresses were no more, thanks to Senator George W. Norris of Nebraska. But when the Congress first met for a full session in January (1934) the Senate leader, Senator Joseph T. Robinson, quickly emerged from a conference with the President, on January 5, saying: "We feel that the situation in Europe is so complex that this is not the opportune time to take up the World Court protocols."

This decision caused surprise, since disposal of the World Court had been expected to be one of the first things done. Naturally there was concern. From Geneva came reports of perplexity and discouragement. It was "felt that if a President as popular as Mr. Roosevelt still feels he cannot get the protocols ratified, and after promising full co-operation with the League drops Court adherence first, all peace disturbers will feel they can be assured that United States co-operation with Geneva in other respects will not be serious."[13]

A few days later President Nicholas Murray Butler, of Columbia University, declared our failure to ratify the Court protocols "the most discreditable thing in the recent history of the United States," and on the twenty-ninth Newton D. Baker, Secretary of War during the Great War, urged that they could be ratified quickly without disturbing the domestic program. Ratification would have a quieting effect upon nations preparing to satisfy their ambitions by war. That the votes were ready was testified by Mrs. Catt on the same day. The women's organizations had made careful check and reported 65 senators, whom she listed by name, as for ratification, 16 opposed and 15 doubtful.

A National Demand for Action. The pressure for action was sufficient to induce a hearing by the Foreign Relations Committee on March 23, 1934. The interest expressed surprised the opposition, which conceded through Borah and Johnson that the protocols would be reported out of the Committee, though probably too late for action during the session. More than three hundred supporters of the Court filled the Senate caucus room for the hearing, which was marshaled by Clarence E. Martin, former president of the American Bar Association. He told how carefully that top organization of American lawyers had considered the Protocol of Adhesion before concluding that it fully met the 1926 reservations. Now, he continued, "it is the deliberate judgment of the American Bar Association that the national honor and welfare require our entrance into the Court." In the name of the Association he added the hope that action would be speedy, a hope strongly voiced by former Governor Alfred E. Smith of New York.

Mr. Henry I. Harriman, president of the Chamber of Commerce of the United States, then told the Committee how often his premier organization of businessmen had urged entry into the Court. He was supported by General Charles R. Sherrill, president of the New York State Chamber of Commerce, and by Dr. S. Parkes Cadman, who spoke for the thirty million people represented in the Federal Council of Churches of Christ in America, whose constituent bodies had so often voiced their sentiments. For ten years, he chided, "the desire of the churches and of a vast number of citizens has been abundantly clear. . . . We urgently press upon the Senate the imperative need of immediate and favorable action on the World Court protocols." In similar vein Mrs. Catt told how 1866 women's organizations had recently adopted resolutions favoring the Court, and she added: "The world needs just now a few gestures toward peace, instead of so many toward war."

Tom Wallace, editor of the Louisville *Times*, spoke for 108 World Court Committees and W. W. Waymack, associate editor of the Des Moines *Register*, presented a recent poll of the press which showed that of 2000 daily newspapers 1367, or two thirds, were editorially supporting adherence to the Court. He submitted the figures state by state, pointing out that most of the opposition centered in the Hearst papers.

The testimony of many others added to the clear evidence of reasoned support by the overwhelming majority of thinking Americans. Ten years of wrangling and obstruction had not budged them. This, however, made no difference to the self-appointed guardians of our national future. After the hearing was concluded Senator Hiram Johnson threatened that if the Court protocols "come before this session of the Senate, the debate will be so bitter and determined as to carry the session into the dog days."[14] So far as Johnson's group was concerned the dog days never ended. The Battalion of Death was always in the manger and never afraid to bark viciously.

As the New York *Times* editor said on the same day, argument for and against American adherence had long since been exhausted. The two political parties had favored our joining the Court again and again, "but their leaders have done nothing about it except recommend." Always there were fears of a long debate, so action must wait until a more convenient season. But, "judging from the past, that season will never come. Successive Congresses and Presidents of both political parties have made a long and painful record of dilatoriness and indifference in this matter."

Opposition Arguments. On May 16 the Senate Committee held a hearing to give the opposition an opportunity to voice its objections. This session was featured by the presentation of a large petition directed against both the League and the Court and bearing the signatures of 1,334,347 persons, whose names had been gathered by the Hearst organizations, sometimes under the pretext that the petition was "against war."[15] Further opposition was expressed by Edward A. Hayes for the American Legion, which had now changed sides, and by Mrs. Lowell Hobart, past president of the D.A.R. Daniel F. Cohalan, of New York, asked if in addition to our great part in the last war we now wished to make an additional contribution of eleven billions in war debts, implying that the World Court would take these debts away from us through an advisory opinion. He did not add that if that were possible it could be done at any time, without our "adherence" to the Court, and without our having any chance of protest or way to forestall it. Referring to the provision for our participation in the election of judges, J. Reuben Clark gravely told the Committee that under the Adhesion Protocol the United States couldn't avoid becoming a partial member of the League of Nations. Evidently this was still believed to be the kiss of death.

The meat of the hearing was the testimony of three former members of the Committee, Otis Glenn, James A. Reed, and G. W. Pepper. They fell back on the perennial hypothetical case technique. Pepper drew out the old bugbear of the Galápagos Islands which Senator Lodge had first thought of in March 1911. Suppose Ecuador should decide to sell them to Japan? Reed raised another ancient ghost: Panama Canal tolls. If this question were raised before the Court every nation owning a ship would have an interest opposed to ours. Therefore every judge of the Court from a nation which owned a ship would vote against the United States. Otherwise he would be a "bad citizen."

By assuming that no judge of the Court could or should rise above the interests of the country in which he was born, Reed reduced the Court to futility. No question of sufficient importance to cause war could come before it in which "each judge" would not have "a deep personal interest," and therefore be disqualified to sit on the case. The probability that a majority of the Court would usually be quite without such interests was ruled out.

Anyway, the World Court did not possess "a single attribute of a court." The judges on it were without "our outlook, principles, constitution, ideas, or philosophy." Their countries had been in "acrimonious and constant dissension" for many centuries. Calmly ignoring his own heavy responsibility for the impotence of the international machinery before Japanese aggression, Reed charged that "the rape of

Manchuria stands unchallenged, despite this so-called Court."[16]

Shelved Again. Finally, on May 31, Senator Robinson presented a resolution to shelve the Court again until January 1935, and then to take it up as the first business of the Committee and press for final action. Afterward Hiram Johnson commented that it would have been "idiotic and simply outrageous to inject the Court into the present session and disrupt what we are all trying to do with regard to the recovery program." Johnson had been re-elected with the President's support and was co-operating on domestic issues, for the moment.

Silence then fell upon our relation to the World Court until November 8, when, at a dinner in New York, Newton D. Baker went to the root of our national sickness. He attacked the system of checks and balances by which the initiative of the executive in foreign affairs is nullified by the veto of the Senate, so that contest for prestige between the two almost paralyzes us into inability to act at all. A pigeonhole in the desk of the Senate Foreign Relations Committee had taken the place of the debate and decision of international issues, and "no one can debate satisfactorily with a pigeonhole."

On the same occasion Raymond D. Fosdick observed, "Posterity will never forgive us if we fail to take any step which might prevent another war." The frustration of an immense desire that the United States should not remain helplessly in that negative position was nearing totality. But would posterity fix responsibility on the relatively few ruthless men who in this crucial matter had imposed their will upon the nation?

In December 1934 it was already too late for the small step of our adherence to the World Court to have any important significance. The obstructionists had done their work too well. Already the Second World War was well begun, though the senators didn't know it. Manchuria was overrun and the Chinese sections of Shanghai had already been subjected to merciless area bombing.

The United States, too, sensing trouble from an unexpected quarter, had actually sent a representative to "sit with" the League Council. He sat, uncomfortably and dumbly, and thereafter the League and the United States took turns in urging each other ahead and in lagging behind, while the Japanese worked their will on the helpless Chinese, and Mussolini prepared his wanton aggression on Ethiopia, now ready to be launched.

The few precious years after 1918 had been irretrievably used up. The chance of a century was gone. The objectors had created imaginary dangers and magnified them into monstrosities, while the ugliest aggressions ever plotted matured under their noses. The men of iron will and endless cunning had prevailed in the Senate, and through it over the rest of humanity. For sixteen years they had successfully blocked and vetoed every step toward bolstering the new institutions of world government before it was too late. Now it was too late for any extremely frigid recognition of the World Court to halt the tidal waves of world gangsterism which were ready to break loose.

But the embattled senators continued to box implacably with that gargantuan shadow, "the possible embarrassment of our rich and upright country through some advisory opinion of the World Court"!

CHAPTER VIII

Defeat

ON January 6, 1935, Hamilton Holt, president of Rollins College, expressed the belief that the World Court would probably have run the gantlet of the Senate successfully at any time in the preceding five years, had it been brought to a vote. "But its enemies were determined and its friends were timid."

There was a considerable degree of truth in this observation, insofar as the Court's political friends were concerned. It could never be taken up when there was anything important to do, or near the end of any session, because the objectors would paralyze everything. All shrank from the ordeal of wearing them down or of imposing the dreaded closure upon them. After all, the Court could wait. Everyone knew that the direct importance of "joining" it was small, and a favorable time would eventually come. In the meantime there was always a strong majority in the Senate for the Court, so there was no cause for alarm.

Finally, in January 1935, the "favorable" moment arrived. A British newspaperman of long experience in Washington wrote later that when Congress met there was little for it to do, so "the President tossed to the Senate the World Court treaty which he expected would be ratified without any trouble."[1] On January 6 the New York *Times* reported that President Roosevelt had "suddenly" called a conference of party leaders, at which it was decided to bring out the Court protocols. There was some feeling that it would be better for the President to remain silently in the background during the fight, and on the twelfth the *Times* stated that not more than twelve senators would vote against the Court. The opposition leaders were discouraged. Nationalistic feeling was quiescent. Senator Charles L. McNary, Republican leader in the Senate, predicted prompt ratification.

Nazi Germany was also impressed by the imminence of our long-delayed entry into the Court. The Berlin *Tageblatt* commented, on the tenth, that it would be a step toward America's ultimate entrance into the League and predicted that if we approved the Court Japan would not complete her resignation from the League. There is a glimpse here of the paralyzing and confusing effect which our entry into the Court and the League—urged in a radio address by Senator James P. Pope of Idaho on the eleventh—might have had even at this late date. Mussolini was already busy organizing the aggression upon Ethiopia to which the League's weakness against Japan had emboldened him. It is not to be supposed, either, that the Nazi dreams of world conquest could have been easily dissolved. On the other hand, the Rhineland occupation, key to all of Hitler's conquests, had not yet taken place, and a vigorous application of pressure, or sanctions, by the League—led by Britain, Russia, and the United States— would have stopped Mussolini in Ethiopia and broken the uninterrupted chain of successful aggressions.

If the greatest powers had united to defend the collective peace, the direction in which the wind was blowing would have been reversed. But Britain was breathing appeasement, and in the United States Senator Gerald P. Nye of North Dakota had already had his Munitions Investigating Committee going full blast for six months, rewriting the history of our entry into the Great War and convincing a majority of Americans that we had fought in that war only because of

Wilson's weakness, plus the cupidity of our bankers and munitions makers. The greatest and most calamitous falsification of history ever achieved was well under way, preparing the ground for the high Washington barricade of paper laws against the next war, each "neutrality" law and flood of speeches telling the aggressors not to mind us. We were out.

Peace through Isolation. A sample of the inverted oratory which was to sweep all before it was supplied by Senator Hiram Johnson on January 13, 1935. After his usual lament about the abandonment of George Washington's policy Johnson asserted that "joining the Court does not mean the promise of peace, but may involve us in a war." The self-destroying idea that union for peace means war was fixed in the minds of the isolationist leaders. They had been driven into this defeatist position by their fight on the League and meant to cling to it until death.

Many Irish-Americans also were still irreconcilable. They had opposed the League as a British concoction and they continued to oppose the League Court. On the thirteenth, eight Irish societies in New York, claiming 100,000 members, sent telegrams to their senators opposing the World Court and urging "political isolation" for the United States. The next day, as the Court issue was brought up in the Senate, Borah served notice that a determined stand would be made against it, and Senator Gore of Oklahoma offered a reservation to withhold adherence until all our war debts had been collected in full, a proposal that was soon to command 26 votes.

Strong Support. Already the signs of opposition impelled the President to send a short message to the Senate, on the sixteenth, in which he stated, "The movement to make international justice practicable and serviceable is not subject to partisan considerations. For years Republican and Democratic Administrations and party platforms alike have advocated a court of justice to which nations might voluntarily bring their disputes for judicial decision." Mindful of what had happened in 1926, the President urged that "the Senate's consent be given in such a form as not to defeat or delay the objective of adherence." Now, he continued, "when every act is of moment to the future peace of the world, the United States has an opportunity once more to throw its weight into the scale in favor of peace."[2]

Editorial opinion also felt strongly that a gesture toward the Court was a step in the right direction. "It may help the world to turn the corner," said the *Christian Science Monitor* on the sixteenth. The same point was made by the Philadelphia *Inquirer*, on the seventeenth, and the Baltimore *Sun* (January 16) urged that "a beginning must be made somewhere, if we are ever to get away from war." It was unthinkable to the Denver *Rocky Mountain News* (January 18) "that the United States, a leader in world peace, should stay out of the established system of international justice." Likewise the Cleveland *Plain Dealer* thought that "America belongs to the World Court just as surely as America esteems the judicial process above the arbitrament of war," and asserted that "it is time for the majority to quit letting itself be kicked around by the minority." The Indianapolis *Star* scored the past action of the Senate as "no credit to the nation" and the Louisville *Courier-Journal* (January 17) wanted the Senate to "make quick work" of brushing the objectors aside and "dispose finally of a matter which should have been disposed of long ago."

The Omaha *World-Herald* (January 16) also branded the opposition as "another 'little group of willful men,' supported on the outside by tom-tom beaters under Hearst leadership, stubbornly bent upon nullifying platform pledges," and the Des Moines *Register* (January 17) demanded that the United States quit "pretending and stalling and ducking and do something definite." The only opposition to the Court had been "a jockeying, delaying, prejudice-fomenting, usurping little minority of chronic antis, backed by a group of chain newspapers that reflect but the personal bias of one man, Mr. Hearst." Similarly, the Milwaukee *Journal* would demand of "any senator who votes against this Court his reasons," and they should "be such as a man can give with a good conscience to the children growing up around us who will be the victims of any war." The inevitable reservations, said the Concord *Daily Monitor and New Hampshire Patriot* (January 17) are "implements of a misguided opposition rather than safeguards of American interests."

Further editorials in support of the Court were printed in the Washington *Evening Star,* the Raleigh *News and Observer,* and the New Orleans *Times-Picayune;* the Phoenix *Arizona Republic* on the eighteenth; the Boise *Capital News* on the nineteenth; and the Nashville *Tennessean* on the twenty-first.

Yet the Detroit *Free Press* (January 19) expressed fear that "America might find itself inside the League and involved in European squabbles, intrigues, and wars," and was strong for reservations. The Reno *Evening Gazette* (January 17) deplored our entry into a Court whose decisions are not based upon "a single elementary principle of justice," and agreed with the Kansas City *Star* (January 17) that the Court's decisions "have been plainly political." The Court was characterized by the Tulsa *Daily World* (January 18) as "a sugar-coated adjunct of the troublesome and ineffectual League," and, as if to settle all argument, the Hearst Seattle *Post-Intelligencer* (January 16) maintained that "nowhere in the world, except among American propagandists for the entanglement of this country with the League, do any self-respecting jurists pretend that the Court is not a part of the League."

Why Go Abroad? As soon as the President's message saying

that we had another opportunity to throw our weight into the scale in favor of peace had been read, Senator Hiram Johnson took the floor to maintain that he wanted peace but "what peace do we gain by going into this Court or by going into the League of Nations?" Going into the Court would "ultimately mean going into the League of Nations just as surely as night follows day." Why enter "to meddle and muddle, under an hysterical internationalism in those controversies that Europe has and that Europe will never get rid of"? This was the worst moment to go into the Court, when "all Europe sits on a volcano" and no one knew when the explosion would come.

Johnson was horrified also at the idea that giving the Court a nod of recognition would mix us up in sanctions when the explosion came. "Sanctions!" he cried. "Sanctions mean simply starvation, want, hunger, killing the weak, the infirm, the small, the aged, and the young—those who cannot fight. They mean the cruelest thing there is in all warfare." Little did Johnson know that these alleged effects of economic sanctions upon an aggressor state would within eight years be exceeded a thousand times over by the results of brutal aggression upon the lives of hundreds of millions of people living on both sides of us—tens of millions wantonly killed, scores of millions sadistically maltreated, hundreds of millions starved and terrorized. While he was deploring the use of a little force in the name of law, to preserve civilization itself, gangster power was swiftly being generated which would grip the world itself by the throat.

But in his speech of January 16, 1935, Johnson celebrated the twenty-first birthday of his grandson, whom he did not want "sent over to China in a war between China and Japan." Under the influence of the "other people's wars" obsession, he did not foresee that within six years his own country would be attacked by Japan, because it could not consent to the creation of a Japanese military empire based on the wealth of all East Asia. In 1935 he magnanimously gave his "hearty assent to the doctrines of the League of Nations and the World Court, so long as they are practiced and so long as they are developed for European ills, but we are different from those people abroad—can you not understand that?" For us Johnson would have none of "this nefarious contraption abroad," because "God gave us two great oceans. . . . We are different over here. Why go abroad?" The idea that we are so much better than other peoples was a strong ingredient in the isolationist delusion.

But wasn't there really some danger in our lending a bit of recognition to the World Court? On that point the senator had no doubts. Thundered Johnson: "Once we have advisory opinions rendered in which the United States is interested, the whole fabric that has been built up since we were a nation goes crumbling to the ground!"[3] Just one advisory opinion and the Republic would be wrecked.

The next day Senator Huey P. Long, the machine-gun ruler of Louisiana, gave the Senate what the press termed "a three-hour harangue." "Waving his arms and shouting at the top of his lungs," he accused the Standard Oil Company, with which he was at war in Louisiana, of financing Bolivia's war against Paraguay. Like Johnson, he stressed the impossibility of a creditor submitting to the judgment of his debtors. Already there was fear of a filibuster. The Court opponents asserted their strength and it was feared that the Administration would have to concede some further reservations.[4] The usual process of emasculation was under way.

The resolution of ratification reported by the Committee on Foreign Relations had been relatively moderate. Since ratification without any reservations would have been wholly unthinkable, it was proposed "with the clear understanding of the United States that the Permanent Court of International Justice shall not, over an objection by the United States, entertain any request for an advisory opinion touching any dispute or question in which the United States has or claims an interest."[5]

This reassertion of the old Reservation 5 in its pristine terms could not avoid being offensive to the members of the Court. It ignored completely the Root formulas so carefully worked out in the Adhesion Protocol and reasserted the original Senate claim, just as if nothing had happened since January 27, 1926. But this blunt reassertion was not, of course, sufficient. Senator Vandenberg was unreconciled to the omission of the sacred Hague Conference words. How could any important treaty be passed without this talisman being attached to it?

The Immortal Reservation Restored. Vandenberg was defeated in the Committee, 11 to 9, on the tenth, but he promptly offered the magic formula in the Senate and the foreordained support developed. No departing by the United States from "its traditional policy of not intruding upon, interfering with, or entangling itself in" political questions, and no relinquishment of its "traditional attitude toward purely American questions!"

In pleading for the inclusion of these charmed phrases Vandenberg admitted that the pending protocol did not infringe upon them, but he could see no reason why senators should object to a mere "reiterated assertion in specific terms of what proponent senators claim to be the unimpaired American status." He was "amazed" that there should be any opposition. That created a "needless doubt" that should be cleared up. "If it is a surplusage, it can do no harm. If it is not a surplusage it is vitally necessary."

This was the old, old argument by which all treaties can be killed, coming or going. If any question has been raised, then ipso facto there must be a reservation about it, just to make sure. But Vandenberg went further. As if suspecting that he was not arguing the most urgent cause imaginable, he continued: "I beg of senators to think of this open-mindedly, because there is a reality in the advisability of this declaration. If the declaration never had been made before in this connection, the situation might be different; but since it has been made heretofore, the affirmative refusal to repeat the declaration today too easily invites what I believe to be the false implication that there is a change in the status from the status of those other occasions."[6]

This was a new refinement in the intricate business of reservation making. A reservation, having been made a time or two, must become immortal. It must be attached to every treaty that comes along or somebody might think there had been a change in our status. The "status" of the United States would be eternal, if only these beloved words were recited on all possible occasions, so they were gravely inserted by the Senate on motion of Senator Robinson, January 24.

The Ancient Double Check against Judicial Settlement Revived. Then another still more ancient ritual remained. The Committee had actually omitted the requirement that nothing should go to judgment without first being scrutinized by the Senate. So Senator George W. Norris of Nebraska introduced a reservation on the twenty-fifth, providing that no dispute should be sent to the Court until the form of its submission had been approved by a two-thirds vote of the Senate. Norris was one of the most respected men in the Senate, but when an important treaty was to be made he became an absolute perfectionist. He admitted that President Roosevelt, in whom he had great confidence, was opposed to his reservation but "if we reject the particular reservation . . . it will have the effect of throwing the matter into the hands of Presidents whom you do not know and whom I do not know, whose sincerity probably would be as unquestioned as that of the present President; but we do not know that to be so."[7]

In other words, President Roosevelt would not sell us out in sending cases to the World Court, but some other President might. That any President, however simple, would invite great unpopularity by such a course might be a very slight possibility, but the future must be totally insured, by leaving all future decisions to the inexhaustible wisdom of the Senate. Our urgent problem of living in the age of robot planes and rocket bombs cannot be solved without recognizing fully the paralyzing effect of this well-meant perfectionism. It lays the hand of death over each important treaty as it enters the Senate, especially if it be a peace treaty with many nations.

In this case the Administration reacted promptly and vigorously. President Roosevelt denounced the Norris reservation at his press conference as a definite limitation on the constitutional powers of the President. Senator Robinson also attacked it in the Senate, pointing out that it would permit the renewal of the controversy then raging every time a dispute was sent to the Court. He placed in the *Record* the history of forty arbitration cases which had been sent to arbitration without any censorship by the Senate,[8] and won the defeat of the Norris reservation, 47 to 37, on the same day it was submitted.

This victory, however, was short-lived. As opposition mounted the Administration became so alarmed that on January 29 Senator Elbert Thomas offered the formula of the 1926 resolution and the 1932 report, no cases to be sent to the Court except through "general or special treaties."

Eternity Not Quite Regulated. This left the bare and exceedingly remote possibility that the Senate might sometime agree to a general arbitration treaty, a prospect which appalled Senator Norris. He at once moved to have the words "general or" stricken out, so as to make absolutely certain that no dispute could go to the Court without a two-thirds vote of the Senate. That would mean that if the dispute was important its reference to the Court would be blocked by the high-voltage America Firsters of the day. The Court "may be different fifty years from now," argued Norris.

Again Norris was defeated, 48 to 39, so just before the final vote he gravely explained that since this tiniest of future loopholes had not been closed he found it to be his conscientious duty to vote against the entire resolution of adherence. He agreed that it was very unlikely that the Senate would ever approve a general arbitration treaty, but his amendment to prevent that faint possibility was "absolutely necessary to save our country from some possible danger," for "there may come controversies after we are dead and gone, if we agree to such a general treaty" of arbitration.[9]

One of the most useful senators on domestic questions which the Senate ever had was not willing to trust anybody in the slightest degree in foreign affairs—neither the good sense and enlightened self-interest of the World Court judges nor the patriotism of any future President of the United States; neither the well-known conservatism of the State Department nor the jealous touchiness of future Senates. The future must be foreclosed absolutely. It must be tied up now for eternity itself, so that no fallible men of the future could determine their own destiny. Wars might come and go and civilization itself might again hang in the balance for long years, as it had from 1914 to 1918, but no dispute could go to the World Court without the all-wise benediction of two thirds of the United States Senate.

How the Perfectionists and Objectors Prevail. The acceptance of the 1926–32 formula on "general or special treaties" by the Administration was at once hailed in the Senate as a retreat, especially since Senator Johnson had fought for that reservation in the Committee and been defeated, 12 to 9. Arthur Krock, veteran Washington observer for the New York *Times,* wrote on January 31 that the kidnaping of the Johnson reservation by the Administration was "a confession of serious weakness during battle and it persuaded several fence sitters to jump down into the opposition field."

This incident of the 1935 defeat illustrates another of the omnipotent weapons in the hands of the objectors to any treaty. They complain—loudly and gently, angrily and persuasively—until some lukewarm senators begin to waver. Then the Administration, growing constantly more alarmed, begins to concede reservations designed to hold senators in line—and the rout is on. The result is likely to be failure to get the two-thirds vote in the end, but, if not, there will be a list of strangling, offensive reservations which will kill the treaty anyway. It is a game in which the objectors can hardly lose. They win either on the final vote in the Senate or a little later when the other nations consider the Senate's ultimatum.

The U. S. A.—Safe from All "Furriners." Before the final blow was delivered in 1935 Senator Borah made a long argument to prove from the Austro-German customs union opinion that the Court was political. "This Court," he maintained, "is not an American product and springs from no American proposal."[10] How you could have an international court that was a pure American product was not explained, but nothing less would satisfy Senator Robert R. Reynolds of North Carolina. Terming the World Court "this Court of intrigue," and stressing heavily that recognizing it meant entering the League, he expanded on the fact that of the fifteen judges only two spoke English! "What chance would we poor Americans have with some fellows there speaking five or six languages?" Our people did not "want any foreign justice. They want American justice," asserted Reynolds, and personally he did not want to mix up with "them furriners."

He had talked to his constituents down in North Carolina and knew that they were not interested in preserving the peace of Ethiopia, in keeping the peace of "countries of which the great majority had never heard. What do my constituents care about spending money and time and energy and life and blood for the interest of Estonia, Ethiopia, Iraq, Latvia, Liberia?" Nothing. "Was the League of Nations a creation of the thought of the people of America? It was not. Why? Because, Mr. President, the United States of America has nothing at issue now, nor will it have anything at issue in the future which will cause us to be at odds with other nations of the world."

That was all there was to it. The United States was perfectly safe, so immune from trouble that we would not even have any disputes with other nations in the future. We could be carefree and untrammeled—except that seven years later "our boys" would be fighting in every part of the world, from the hottest to the coldest, to prevent two gangster empires from closing in on the North American continent. They would be fighting not to enforce the decisions of a League of Nations Council when aggression was still young and relatively easy to deal with, but after the gangster empires were on the verge of mastering the labor and resources of half a billion people on each side of us. Then we fought, not at the cost of hundreds of millions of dollars, but at the sacrifice of hundreds of billions, and of great casualties instead of small ones.

Blitz Attack on the Senate. As the struggle in the Senate drew to a close that body was subjected to its first blitz propaganda assault. For ten years all manner of organizations and individuals had petitioned the Senate in favor of the World Court, but this was something different. It was the same kind of raging, tearing campaign which had worked up popular fury against the League of Nations, only it was concentrated into a few days. Huey Long led it in the Senate; William Randolph Hearst whipped it up in his great chain of newspapers; and Charles E. Coughlin stirred it to white heat over the air.

Each of this trio was an expert dealer in hate, but the latter was the most bizarre. Coughlin had developed as a Catholic priest a capacity to charm and stir people by his radio talks from Detroit on an extensive chain. His main stock in trade was a muddled radicalism, lambasting the plutocrats and demanding "social justice." He founded a weekly magazine, *Social Justice,* which steadily edged toward fascism until it was banned from the mails as subversive, after Pearl Harbor. As Coughlin's power grew, also, he expanded into the international field as a rabid isolationist.

At the psychological moment he struck. On January 20 he roared: "The plain truth is that Europe has a debt question to settle, and that Europe is philosophically and nationally prepared to gang us into submission."[11]

On the night of the twenty-seventh, with a vote on the Court impending on the twenty-ninth, Coughlin's impassioned voice burned the air waves, imploring and commanding "every solid American who loves democracy, who loves the truth, to stand foursquare back of those tried and true senators of long experience in their hopeless yet honest fight to keep America safe for Americans and not the hunting ground of international plutocrats." He urged his listeners to telegraph their senators immediately—"whether you can afford it or not, send your senator a telegram telling him to vote no on our entrance into the World Court with or without reservations." War had been waged ever since the Court was organized, he said, and the World Court had done nothing to end or prevent the wars. "Thus the World Court has demonstrated that it has no power to keep peace in the world."[12]

This appeal to action was supported by galvanic stimuli such as: "*The so-called World Court is a double-headed tiger born of the League of Nations. It is part and parcel of it . . . and will eventuate in the pilfering of twelve billion dollars from the American people!*" And again: "The League of Nations and its perverted brain the World Court is nothing more than a Frankenstein, raised by the international bankers and the plutocrats of the world for the purpose of preserving by force of arms that plutocratic system against the possible onslaughts of communism!"

Later Coughlin was to make communism the great enemy, but at the moment it was a quasi ally. "Here is this great World Court," he fulminated, "which has a colorless flag, an acreless domain, and the sovereignty of martial forces and at its command the troops of the world, for the purpose of carrying out its decisions." This jumble of falsehoods would not impress anyone who knew his world politics, but to millions of simple people who read the Hearst press and the Chicago *Tribune* it sounded alarming and was infuriating.

Wavering Senators Surrender. In reply to Coughlin, Senator Robinson went on the air, as did Mrs. Franklin D. Roosevelt, Senator Bailey, Newton D. Baker, and Monsignor John A. Ryan, a distinguished Catholic scholar. But all these people spoke in the language of facts and reason. The great majority of their hearers probably assented and approved, but they did not rush to the telegraph offices. Coughlin's followers did. They launched a tidal wave of telegrams at a relatively small number of doubtful senators. Forty thousand telegrams scorched the wires to Washington in a single day, with plenty more the next day, swamping the telegraph companies. Messenger boys staggered into the offices of the wavering senators, dumped their loads of blistering messages, and went back for more.

Senators were impressed. The voice of the people was speaking. They didn't stop to ask whether it was the voice of reason or of impulse. And they forgot entirely the numerous millions of solid, responsible people who for many years had soberly urged upon them our adherence to the Court. The Court's supporters, being moderate people, probably would not punish senators at the polls, but here was the authentic voice of passion and vindictiveness.

To help make it effective the Hearst press pulled out all stops, urging telegrams to senators, quoting sarcastic accounts of the Senate debate by Will Rogers, a much-loved humorist who urged that what we needed was "moral leadership at home," putting people to work, "instead of dallying with the League Court in a time like this."[13] The opposition press also filled their headlines with great streamers reporting "gag rule" in the Senate, when actually a rule limiting debate had been adopted by unanimous consent. But how were readers to know?

Strong emotion was reflected in the resolutions adopted by several legislatures. The House of Representatives of Nebraska was "unalterably opposed." The legislature of Delaware said it was "inadvisable and detrimental for this nation to participate in the affairs of the League of Nations and other foreign entanglements." The Wisconsin solons sent two separate resolutions, charging that adhering to the Court was "merely entering the League of Nations by the back door . . . whereas we are a self-contained and self-sustained nation consuming over 92 per cent of our own produce and do not need to fawn upon other nations for economic and political favors." It would be easy to become subservient to the League of Nations, "whereas our participation in the World War, with its ghastly cost in lives and money and shattered hopes, was a sufficient lesson to us to stay far away from foreign strife."[14] The thesis of the group of young senators whose fathers had unsuccessfully opposed our part in the Great War had taken firm root in Wisconsin, as elsewhere. It had not been our war. We had only blundered and been inveigled into it.

The Minority Wins Again. Before these resolutions could reach the Senate it had voted on the Court protocols and defeated them, January 29, 1935, by a vote of 52 for to 36 against. Forty-three Democrats and nine Republicans voted for adherence; twenty Democrats, fourteen Republicans, and two others voted nay. A strong majority still stood by the Court, but seven votes were lacking to make the required two thirds. The blitz campaign of the impassioned objectors had swung just enough votes to defeat the Court, by exactly the same lack of votes which had defeated the League of Nations Covenant.

The Menace of the Treaty Veto Seen. Succeeding press comment revealed a growing realization of the danger to the nation in the two-thirds vote for treaties requirement. Both the Washington *Evening Star* (January 30) and the Washington *Post* (January 31) pointed out that the minority dominated. "The tail wags the dog." The Hartford *Daily Times* (January 30) made the same point and thought it "most deplorable that prejudice and fear have won a victory impugning the good sense of the nation." "It is perhaps not to be wondered at," said the Baltimore *Sun*, "that the Senate's obscurantists, aided and abetted by an amazing assortment of clowns and professional patriots on the outside, have triumphed again. Once more the easy bombast of the rabble rousers has prevailed over the sober judgment of every President of the United States since Woodrow Wilson, and the resolution of adherence to the World Court, crippled and emasculated though it was, has again been rejected." It was a "new exhibition of narrowness and ignorance made possible by a regrettable provision of our Constitution." Because of its "unworkable treaty system," said the Des Moines *Register* (January 30), the United States is unable "to make any promise to any nation that can be counted on to be kept," and the Montgomery *Advertiser* (February 3) added that "it is a matter of speculation as to whether any measure could pass the Senate by a two-thirds vote regardless of its nature."

The Richmond *Times-Dispatch* (January 31) termed the vote "a tragedy not only for this country but for the world," the triumph of "prejudice and passion over reason and intelligence." The Little Rock *Arkansas Gazette* (January 31) deplored the "phobia" of the opposition and the Indianapolis *Star* (January 31) was perturbed by the success of "misleading propaganda of agitators" in swaying votes in the Senate. The Sacramento *Union* (January 30) attributed the defeat to "a determined stand by a few irreconcilables" and "the heat of prejudice." The Portland *Oregonian* (January 31) regretted that "counsels of selfishness and timidity again have prevailed" and warned that war among other peoples was quite likely to mean war for us. Likewise looking ahead, the Cleveland *Plain Dealer* (January 30) observed that in the long run the defeat would not "loom as large as it does to-day." Another rebuff only served to remind us "that Woodrow Wilson marched with the advance in his concepts of international comity. Someday the world will catch up with his ideals, even including two thirds of the members of the American Senate."

Newspapers which rejoiced over the defeat of the Court, in addition to the Hearst press, included: the Boston *Post,* the Bangor *Daily News,* and the Memphis *Commercial Appeal* (January 30); the Chicago *Tribune* and the Detroit *Free Press* (January 31).

Why the Minority Ruled. Apart from the towering reason for our failure to support the World Court—the two-thirds vote—we failed in 1935 partly because of lax management on the part of the Court's friends. Debate had been allowed to drag in the Senate. Some alleged that a vote was not pushed because the Administration's legislative program was not ready. In any event, time was given for the opposition to rouse the passions upon which it relied and to hurl them at the doubtful senators.

Meanwhile the objectors dominated the floor in the Senate. This was partly because everything that could be said on a basis of reason had been said so many times already. But it was partly because of lack of organization on the Court side. Senator Robinson, majority leader, did well in replying to the opposition, but no one else did much. Senators Elbert Thomas and James P. Pope made excellent speeches for the Court, models of reasonable statement, yet they both indicated that they were acting entirely on their own. The majority of the Foreign Relations Committee was not organized into an alert, aggressive team. On the contrary, the Democratic chairman, Senator Key Pittman of Nevada, was so nearly hostile that he spoke only briefly and rarely. Robinson had to do what he could alone.

The public generally thought that the result could not be in doubt. The President's prestige was great and the mind of the nation had long been made up. Only two days before the vote the New York *Times* said editorially, on the twenty-seventh, that there has "never been a doubt, especially since President Roosevelt's message, that two thirds of the Senate would favor ratification," though it was added that Roosevelt was "puzzled" by the devious ways of the opposition in fighting the treaty. This state of mind in the White House recalled President Coolidge's discovery that the Senate was "a very curious body."[15]

Immediately after the defeat Senator Robinson wrote an article about the struggle in which he said that some fifteen senators who were friendly to ratification, but not unqualifiedly committed, ended by joining the opposition, while only two votes not counted upon were picked up. He ascribed the result to the organized resistance, which daily gathered volume, and to its "exaggerations, misinformation, political threats, and misrepresentations." Pictures were painted "of battle scenes, death, desolation, and sacrifices to accomplish purposes in no wise related to the welfare of our people."[16]

The vote in the Senate reflected: (1) the success of a violent, unscrupulous opposition; (2) the failure of the Court's friends in the Senate to put up an organized, vigorous fight for ratification, fighting steadily instead of yielding ground constantly; and (3) an undoubted revulsion of many people away from the gathering storms abroad. The isolationists preached false tidings, but they offered escape by retreat into our own supposedly ample shell. Senator William G. McAdoo of California, a chief lieutenant of Woodrow Wilson, returned from Europe on February 1 and explained that, though formerly for the League of Nations, he was now against any "foreign entanglements." We could contribute nothing to peace. Europe was now armed to the teeth. It was wise for us to maintain a position of independence. Said McAdoo with finality: "They have fundamental difficulties and problems in which we have no conceivable part."

The catastrophic delusion of the appeasing thirties was packed into that one sentence. Go to the aid of Ethiopia and get ourselves into trouble? Stop Hitler from militarizing the Rhineland? He was just fortifying his own territory! Prevent the murder of the Spanish Republic and halt the spread of fascist aggression in its tracks? Fight for Czechoslovakia, "a land of which we know little"? Oppose Japan firmly in the Far East? Why, she would attack the Dutch Indies! Always the piecemeal destruction of every free man's safety was something far away, "in which we have no conceivable part."

Hence the defeat of the World Court in 1935 did not cast gloom on the capital. Arthur Krock reported that congressional leaders, including Senator Robinson, went serenely about their business. At the White House, also, the President seemed to his semiweekly press visitors "to be sincerely unconcerned about the action of the Senate. Nothing like a pall hung over official Washington."[17] The pall was to come a little later, on December 7, 1941. It was to be a great cloud of black smoke, heavy with the acrid fumes of a fine American air force suddenly destroyed on the ground, and of a greater battle fleet blasted while at anchor in harbor.

CHAPTER IX

Into the Abyss

THE DEFEAT of the World Court in 1935 quickened the stampede of the American people into the cellars of isolation. If the Court had been brought up in the succeeding years it would have received a smaller vote each time.

On August 31, 1935, as Mussolini plunged toward the conquest of Ethiopia, our first neutrality law was enacted. It applied an arms embargo impartially to all future belligerents. No distinction between aggressors and victims. A Munitions Control Board to license exports was set up and our citizens warned not to travel on the ships of any belligerent except at their own risk. No going to war again because our people got themselves killed. Even the President retreated to George Washington, declaring at San Diego on October 2, 1935: "Despite what happens in continents overseas, the United States shall and must remain—as long ago the Father of our Country prayed that it might remain—unentangled and free."

The Administration tried to discourage the shipment of war materials to Italy, but on November 15 Secretary Hull had to confess that they had increased instead of diminished. Yet the Congress firmly rejected his plea for discretion in levying embargoes. The second neutrality law, adopted late in February 1936, forbade any belligerents to borrow money in the United States. The Nye Munitions Committee campaign had established moneylending as a leading reason why we entered the last war, so that "road to war" was firmly barricaded. An apparent exception from the law's coldly impartial terms exempted Latin-American countries from the provisions, provided they were not co-operating with a non-American state or states. If they joined their fellow League members in military sanctions against Italy they would also be embargoed.

Eyes Shut to Aggression. Then the fascist governments of Italy and Germany planned the conquest of the Spanish Republic, and when their invasion of Spain was well begun our government adopted the British-French "non-intervention" policy. Most exporters were persuaded not to ship arms to the legal government of Spain. When one did, the President denounced this "unpatriotic" action and the Congress hastily passed a joint resolution, on January 7, 1937, specifically forbidding the shipment of arms to Spain until the civil-war loophole in our neutrality defenses could be plugged. One lone member of the entire Congress voted no. A friendly, liberal government with a splendid program of domestic reform was denied the long-established right to purchase arms for its own defense. It was classed with its fascist invaders and conquerors, who were permitted for two years to butcher their way to the final subjection of Spain, as indignation mounted in the United States until the public-opinion polls all showed a strong majority for the repeal of the Spanish embargo. But it was not repealed. To the bloody end the blackest blot on the diplomatic record of the Roosevelt Administrations remained in full force.

On May 1937 the third neutrality law added new sheets to our system of paper defenses. The President was given authority to permit the sale of a long list of war materials on a strict "cash and carry" basis. With American vessels rigidly excluded from any zones Hitler might wish to fight in, and cash collected for whatever the British and French took away, our neutrality would be secure.

Quarantining Aggressors Rejected. On October 5, 1937, the President momentarily escaped from the heavy blankets of rigid neutrality. Encouraged by friendly contact with the crowds on a long trip, he wrote into his Chicago speech some sentences not scrutinized by his conservative advisers on foreign affairs. He actually spoke of "quarantining" warlike powers. Isolationists everywhere took instant alarm. Their reaction was so intense that in his fireside talk of October 12 the President spoke only of co-operating with the other signatories of the Nine-Power Treaty, "including China and Japan." Friendly Senator Pepper explained "quarantine" as merely letting a troubled area alone, but powerful Senator George of Georgia served stern warning that he would not vote for any measure which would enable the President "to declare who is the aggressor, to say nothing about quarantining the aggressor, because, in my judgment, when we take that stand, we take a step toward war."[1]

Panic When the Japs Sink the Panay. The Japanese knew that the Brussels Conference to consider what to do about the Japanese invasion of China could do nothing against the fiats of the American isolationists. Some Japanese airmen thought it quite safe to sink the American gunboat *Panay* on the Yangtze River, December 12, 1937, and their judgment was at once vindicated. The isolationists in Washington rushed pell-mell for a new cellar. They forced out of a House committee the Ludlow resolution to require a national referendum before war could be declared, "unless our territory were directly invaded." The Hearst press and several misguided peace societies chimed in—notably the National Council for the Prevention of War and the Women's International League for Peace and Freedom—and the Administration had all it could do to defeat the resolution in the House. Instead of standing up against Japan, the congressional isolationists made a powerful drive to make it impossible either for themselves or any future Congress to accept war until bombs were raining on our own heads.

There was a storm of demands that we retire from the Far East and have no truck with the British in the Orient or elsewhere. Hitler's legions conquered Austria (March 11, 1938) without drawing any American condemnation. Our attention turned to weaning Mussolini away from Hitler, a hope which did not die until June 10, 1940, the day he struck France in the back. Yet Secretary Hull manfully denounced isolation and warned of war ahead, on June 3 and August 16, 1938, and on August 18 the President assured Canada that we would "not stand idly by if domination of Canadian soil is threatened."

This hint that the dictators could not count us out entirely aroused so much protest and uneasiness that the President felt compelled himself to retreat to the cellar. His secretary, Stephen Early, emphasized that we had no moral commitments to support the European democracies and the President denounced those who had conveyed the impression that we were a part of a "stop Hitler" movement. They were "one hundred per cent wrong."

With this assurance Hitler proceeded to make the Nuremberg speech of September 9 which doomed Czechoslovakia to national extinction and sent Prime Minister Chamberlain flying to Germany to arrange the terms. The agony of spirit in the United States was intense. "Save Czechoslovakia" meetings were held, but it was left to others to do the saving. No one in authority dared to suggest that there was no chance of halting further aggression unless the United States joined other Great Powers in a firm pledge to resist the next grab with their full power.

But instead the Congress refused to vote money for the defense of Guam. The Japanese might be offended. There was an outcry because a French officer was killed in a flying accident in California. Our military secrets were being sold! As Hitler openly made ready to obliterate Poland a secret meeting of congressional leaders was held in the White House, on January 31, 1939. The President tried to explain how serious the situation was. Someone told the press that he had said our frontier is on the Rhine. Damning, entangling phrase! "Some boob thought that one up," said the President on February 3, emphasizing that our policy had not changed and was not going to change. It was still "no entangling alliances." The isolationists had succeeded in giving another green light to Hitler.

Paper Barricades Sufficient. As the zero hour drew near the Administration made another effort to modify the effects of the neutrality laws, especially the arms embargo. But the Bloom bill was unrecognizable after it had been battered in the House and on July 11, 1939, the Senate Committee on Foreign Relations refused, 12 to 11, to consider neutrality revision. Another White House conference was held on July 18, in which the President described for an hour the imminence of a general war. But Senator Borah calmly informed the conference that there would be no war. He had his own sources of information, which proved later to be subscriptions to some English newsletters and tipster sheets. His sources, he declared, had often proved more reliable than the State Department's predictions. Borah's authority was accepted and the President was forced to let Hitler touch off a general war without any restraining hand.

Just after the July conference at the White House the isolationist domination of our foreign policy took a strange turn. Suddenly one of the leading isolationists on the Senate Foreign Relations Committee, Senator Vandenberg, secured the assent of that Committee to a resolution advising the State Department to give Japan the six months' notice required for abrogating our commercial treaty of 1911 with her. The Vandenberg resolution, accepted by the Senate on July 18, also called for the reassembly of the Brussels Conference of 1937 on the Far East. Coming from one who sternly opposed lifting the arms embargo, this looked contradictory, but actually it was a delaying move to sidetrack the strong pressure of public opinion for ending the trade in war materials with Japan, and to get concerted action with Britain and France if any action was to be taken, which was most improbable since these powers were riveted down by Hitler's challenges. Therefore all action by us would probably be avoided, at least for six months.[2]

The Vandenberg resolution thus invited a war in the Pacific at the same time that the Foreign Relations Committee refused to lift the arms embargo against our friends in Europe. "It would be hard," says Walter Lippmann, "to find a more perfect example of total incompetence in guiding the foreign relations of a people. . . . This monstrous imprudence was what passed for foreign policy."[3] The "neutrality" laws were not revised. Hitler invaded Poland on September 1 and devastated her from end to end on the first day. Then, as no important fighting developed between Germany and the Franco-British Allies, Senator Borah termed the war "phony," and former President Herbert Hoover, appraising the strength of the Allies on October 3, saw no "possibility that they can be defeated." They control the seas, said Hoover, and can "sit there until their enemies are exhausted." At the worst there would be a stalemate. "Even if Russia and Italy joined Germany in actual warfare the Allies would still retain control of the seas." Germany might try a quick, overwhelming attack, he added, but there was "little reason to believe it can succeed." Therefore "we need to keep cool. For after all we must keep out of this war. We would be yielding the last stand of democracy if we got into it, win or lose."[4]

The United States reacted into a correct and frigid neutrality and into denouncing the Russian war on Finland, until Hitler invaded Denmark and Norway, on April 8, 1940, and Holland and Belgium on May 9. Then for the first time there was no isolationist offensive to force the executive to walk in the straight paths of neutrality. The isolationist belief in the impregnability of France and Britain weakened and disappeared as France disintegrated and quit the war, leaving Britain standing across twenty miles of water, with her arms left behind at Dunkirk. Deep anxiety gripped us about the fate of the British Navy, if Britain fell. The President started arms across the ocean to Britain, from government stocks. Compulsory military service was adopted and on September 2 the historic exchange of fifty obsolete destroyers for a dozen valuable military bases on British soil was consummated.

Minding Our Own Business. Britain held, and as we armed the hope grew that the British and their Allies could do the fighting while we acted as the arsenal of democracy. This was the theory behind the Lend-Lease Bill, March 11, 1941, the President's own way around all the isolationist prohibitions against lending money to the Allies.

Then as Lend-Lease aid began to grow in volume and German submarines began to resist its flow by attacks on our ships everywhere—the much-feared attacks which caused little excitement when they occurred—the main prohibitions of the neutrality law were repealed. The Senate Foreign Relations Committee acted by the usual 12–11 vote and repeal was accomplished November 7, 1941, 50–37, and in the House by a vote of 212 to 194, after a hard fight. American ships could be armed again, they could sail through belligerent zones and into the ports of our friends who had been holding back the deluge of barbarism singlehanded for a year and a half. The ships carried, furthermore, American arms and supplies of every kind free of monetary considerations. Strong pledges to release economic intercourse from tariff and other shackles were exacted, and—most revolutionary of all—the Lend-Lease Act bound all signatories to defend each other against aggression, with no time limit on the obligation.

The mills of the gods of war had ground very slowly, but they had eventually pulverized even the hard stones of isolationist insistence that aggression in an ever-shrinking world was not "our business."

A fortnight later Japan demanded that we stop our infinitely cautious cessation of aid to her conquest of East Asia and when we refused to agree to recognize her conquest of the Orient she struck the blow at Pearl Harbor, the reports of which Senator Nye at first greeted as an Administration trick. He was so busy fighting a last rear-guard action against being "involved" again in European entanglements that he could not believe he had been struck from an entirely different direction.

Safety without Responsibility. How was it possible for the intelligent American people, after watching the inexorable spread of the First World War until we ourselves were fully engaged, to believe the assurances of the isolationist leaders that all we had to do was to selfishly "mind our own business"? Lippmann explains the paradox on the ground that President Wilson gave legalistic, moralistic, and idealistic reasons for our entry into the Great War, instead of stressing the underlying reason that our security demanded the defeat of Germany's effort to starve Great Britain and take control of the Atlantic Ocean.[5]

There is weight in this contention, though there is more force in Lippmann's thorough demonstration that President Monroe deceived the nation for a century by refusing to promulgate the Monroe Doctrine in alliance with Great

Britain, when it had originated in London and could only be enforced by the British Navy. After the contemporaries and successors of Monroe had inculcated in us for a hundred years the illusion that we enforced the Doctrine, untrammeled and free of all entangling alliances, it would have been indeed an undertaking for Wilson suddenly to kill the teaching of our entire national history and lead us into the war on the cold basis of power politics. But he did hold clearly before us the definite practical objective of joining with all like-minded nations to prevent the pitiable disruption of the peace by future aggression, by extending the Monroe Doctrine to the whole world.

It was this urgent, compelling, wholly demonstrated need which Wilson kept constantly before us, and we cannot say that we did not see the need and recognize the validity of the remedy. For a brief period at the close of the war and after it, the common people of this country knew that obligations to join with other peoples in resistance to aggression were imperatively required. But they allowed themselves to be divided and deceived by the interminable campaign in the Senate against "Wilson's League," and by the double-dealing promises of Wilson's opponents in the electoral campaign of 1920.

Thereafter blind leaders of intense obstinacy led increasing numbers of the blind. Negation was in the saddle and it rode backward from one frustration to another. When the indispensable objective of common action against future aggression was blocked, then the pale substitute of "adherence" to the World Court was brought out, only to be alternately put into frigid storage and hammered about as if it were a cunning and dangerous "contraption."

Then the "outlawry" of war was advanced as a substitute for the substitute, and great numbers of good people clutched at this as a straw which might be of some little use in the next storm. Others promoted outlawry as a final sop to the uneasy conscience of the nation.

The Outlawry of War: Substitute for a Substitute. There is no doubt whatever that Samuel O. Levinson, a successful corporation lawyer of Chicago, was sincerely shocked by his discovery during the First World War that there was no law against war. Here was a world-wide breakdown of all law and order. Many nations were fighting each other, tooth and nail, killing, ravaging, squandering accumulated wealth —a perfect bedlam of anarchy on a world scale. Yet Levinson searched in vain for any international laws against war. Surely there were some prohibitions against such stupendous disorder, some rules, some general understanding to the contrary. But to his astonishment he discovered that war was a perfectly legal, respectable institution. Far from forbidding it, international lawyers accepted it as the most important of all human customs and spent most of their time and thought in constructing rules of warfare that would mitigate its devastating effects a little.

It was not true that international lawyers liked war. Some had always denied its legality, but the majority accepted it as a fixed, unavoidable evil and built their writings around it. A considerable number also, especially in powerful states, accepted it without reluctance as the natural and permanent method of settling serious disputes.

Thus Levinson found that a nation could go to war for any reason, lofty or base, or for no reason, without losing any respectability or incurring any penalties, beyond those of defeat. This was a situation so plainly wrong that he set out to do something about it, and the fact that he was tackling a large order did not deter him. He had tried single-handed for many months to stop the war itself, through influential individuals on both sides. In that he failed, but he would outlaw war.

To this large undertaking Levinson brought remarkable powers. He was one of the most dynamic and energetic of men, tireless, optimistic, resourceful, indomitable. Quite probably he was the greatest propagandist of his age. The fire of the ancient Hebrew phophets burned in him and it seldom burned low. He was in intense, feverish eruption much of the time.

For a brief two months, also, from December 1918 to the evening of February 14, 1919, Levinson supported President Wilson's campaign to achieve a League of Nations, based on the principle of common action against aggression. At the moment the League Covenant was published he was on his way to Washington to line up the objecting Republican senators for the League. But the Covenant chilled him, probably because it left some possible loopholes for war to occur legally. Certainly there was nowhere in it a plain, simple law against all war. Levinson was also a strong Republican partisan and he emerged from his conferences with Knox, Borah, and other bitter-enders as one of them, and as an active brain which provided them many ideas. He agreed with them that Republican prospects for 1920 were excellent, unless there was a split over the League or it gave "the Democrats sufficient prestige to overcome their other handicaps."[6]

For the next ten years Levinson was in constant communication with the Senate irreconcilables, especially Borah, urging, praising, exhorting, pleading that they proceed toward outlawry. Once he persuaded Borah to introduce, on February 13, 1923, a strong resolution, with twelve supporting "whereases," to make war "a public crime under the law of nations" and to provide "that a judicial substitute for war should be created (or, if existing in part, adapted and adjusted) in the form or nature of an international court" with power to decide "all purely international controversies." Enforcement was, however, to be only through the "enlightened power of public opinion."

For six years thereafter Levinson used all of his unusual abilities on Borah to induce him to take up this resolution and make a great speech in its behalf, but in vain. Borah was always wary. However, in the effort to enlist him Levinson spent much of his own money in broadcasting Borah's isolationist utterances. He paid for and distributed 1,100,000 copies of Borah's two speeches of January 22 and 27, 1926, against the World Court, a distribution which must have had appreciable effect on public opinion, and a constant stream of pamphlets, speakers, and other means of influencing opinion issued from his office.[7]

There was a brief period, beginning in November 1924, when Levinson stopped fighting the World Court, during a series of peace conferences with the advocates of the League of Nations, led by James T. Shotwell, but Borah and others "who valued outlawry for its obstructive uses only" were at once miffed, and remained unmollified by Levinson's explanations that he was conferring in order to "intrinsically revolutionize" the Court as a "Republican proposal for peace," instead of leaving it "a mere Democratic resolution to enter that subsidiary of the League."[8] Hence the harmony conferences were abortive. The outlawry school returned to adamant opposition to the World Court and continued to oppose it until after the Pact of Paris was adopted in 1929. Then Levinson gave the Court some support, as a defense of outlawry, but his conversion came too late to repair the damage his great crusade had done. His powerful propaganda in the preceding ten years had been an important influence in fortifying and increasing the opposition to the Court and the League. Levinson had supplied brains and ideas which went a considerable way to prevent the opposition from appearing to be merely negative.

Levinson's success in achieving the Briand-Kellogg Treaty was a gain for the cause of peace. It was time that the nations should all agree to "condemn recourse to war for the solution of international controversies, and to renounce it as an instrument of national policy in their relations with one another." It was eminently fitting that they should promise that "the settlement or solution of all disputes or conflicts of whatever nature or of whatever origin they may be, which may arise among them, shall never be sought except by pacific means."

Toothless Law. The law was splendid. Of itself it later cramped the style of the aggressors somewhat. But it was folly to leave it unsupported by strong institutions of world government, legislative, executive, and judicial. Yet Levinson could not break with the shibboleths of sovereignty and isolation enough to make his law effective. He agreed that armed force might sometime have to be used against a "mad dog" state, but insisted, in 1928, that it was "inconceivable" that anything of the sort would actually happen and that it was bad psychology to keep talking about the possibility. He wrote that "the United States would be the first perhaps to resent insolent breaking of the peace by Mussolini," but when the time came we let aggression run through the whole gamut of insolence and butchery, from Manchuria to Dunkirk, before we bestirred ourselves.

Levinson agreed with Borah that Hamilton had been right in saying that to coerce a state "is one of the maddest projects ever devised . . . a dream . . . impossible." You could not, Levinson argued, put France to death, imprison or starve her. He was unaware that soon France would be imprisoned, tortured, starved until great numbers of her people died, while her movable wealth was carted out of the country year after year. He did not know that the Nazis would systematically put the French nation to death by keeping its manhood in Germany, while every other effort was made to reduce the French people to the status of weak agricultural serfs to the German master race. Nor did he foresee that the Jews of Europe would be murdered, by every means the mind of man could devise, that wholesale efforts would be made to destroy the leaders of the Poles, Serbs, and Greeks and to reduce the numbers of these peoples to such an extent that they could not live as nations, even if freed again. He did not know that he would live to see dozens of nations completely coerced, with all the sadistic brutality that the diseased and primitive minds of immense fascist gangs could devise.

Far from envisaging the coercion of any national state, Levinson rejected the enforcement of his law against war and relied on good faith, public opinion, and non-recognition of conquests to make it effective. He insisted that "our hands must be free,"[9] and free they remained until all hands in the United States had to be mobilized to save the world from anarchy far more terrible and destructive than had ravaged the world from 1914 to 1918.

Immovable International Lawyers. Levinson, however, made more progress than many of the international lawyers whom he had set out to rescue from their tacit alliance with war. Though there were many outstanding exceptions, a large proportion of the older teachers of international law had studied that subject as a millennial science, something which was slowly developing through ages eternal. They took the national state for granted as the last word in human organization. That meant, of course, that war was a part of the natural order of things, to be slowly, ever so slowly, regulated and civilized. They expected progress, in terms of centuries, but nothing more.

The conservative international lawyers believed that things were just that way. You accepted them and encouraged a tiny advance now and a very small reform later on. It was a process almost geologic in its majesty. An atom of good conduct would develop in this age, another rule would be added to "the law" in the next generation, and thus bit by bit refractory humanity would be civilized. It was a comfortable doctrine, one which dignified its holders by the consciousness of stately passage down the stream of time, helping to guide it, not too much but a little.

This atomic growth of international law was rudely shattered by the First World War. So much anarchy could not be reconciled with any sane idea of law. Most people refused to make the effort. The high priests of international law were shocked and wounded. The current events were bad, but to deny that "the law" existed! Hadn't there been other general wars, and hadn't the law resumed its millennial growth afterward?

It was into these wounds of injured pride that the great movement to enforce the peace cast wormwood and gall. Here were people talking about forbidding war, about regulating and controlling the conduct of sovereign nations, about international government! The conservative lawyers were deeply shocked by this misguided movement. Of course it would fail. You had to leave these things to the centuries. And yet, if the League of Nations should succeed in creating real world law, and in enforcing it, the accustomed world of the international lawyers would be destroyed. They would have to wrench themselves loose from the exposition of the slow growth of custom into law and wrestle with the stupendous problems involved in the operation of an international society. It was too much for some. They preferred to remain at the old stand and oppose these newfangled innovations.

The same school was also hurt by the way the First World War thrust the Hague Conferences into the background.

These gatherings, with their very moderate accomplishments, were more in line with the millennial, atomic development of international law.

Thus we had the remarkable spectacle that some international lawyers worked not only against the League of Nations but also refused to welcome the World Court. Instead of regarding it as an epochal advance to be hailed with joy, they regarded it with jaundiced eye and, at the best, took no part in the struggle to see it born. Others fought it constantly.

The traditional lawyers, too, were similarly upset by the Pact of Paris. It was to them the final blow to forbid war altogether and thus destroy at one stroke the bulk of their beloved law. Such fantasy! But it wouldn't last. As the League was eventually challenged successfully by predatory regimes their speeches and writings betrayed satisfaction and relief, and when mounting aggression appeared to reduce the outlawry of war to a nullity there was something like exultation. Pleased speeches at learned societies indicated that if now we could just restore the custom of declaring war, so unwisely interrupted by the Pact of Paris, all would be well. Nor has the Second World War convinced all of the international lawyers that times have really changed. Far from admitting that war must be controlled if civilization is to survive, Edwin Borchard still boldly ascribes the war itself to the foolish attempts at "collective security," with their threat of "sanctions."*

Fortunately the view that our approach to world order must be strictly millennial was not held by the vast majority of American lawyers. The American Bar Association

*See Borchard, "The Place of Law and Courts in International Relations," *American Journal of International Law* (January 1943), pp. 46–57. The "romantic demand" for enforcing peace "has helped to split the world into irreconcilable camps." The attempt to enforce international law "by conjuring up an impossible 'international police' or inventing an imaginary 'collective security,'

passed resolutions favoring our having a part in the World
Court in 1922, 1923, 1929, 1931, and 1934. Underlying this
often repeated national verdict there were resolutions passed
by 62 local bar associations and 35 state bar associations,
many of them repeatedly. The Virginia, Mississippi, and Ohio
bar associations supported the World Court three times;
those of Kentucky, Texas, and New Jersey four times, and
the Bar Association of New York on nineteen occasions. The
nation's lawyers left no doubt of their willingness to support
the World Court and to trust it.[10]

Like the bar associations, the average layman can see for
himself that the ever more rapid destruction of time and
space is welding the world itself into one community. The
First World War proved that for purposes of trade and
war the world was already a unit, and each succeeding day
has increased our power to destroy each other. The slow
evolution of all things has been accelerated to a pace that
is perilous in the extreme. The progressively more rapid advance of science and invention has placed the life of every
nation, none excepted, in imminent peril. The race is on
between the lightning development of all manner of mar-

supported as it is by revival of the discredited and unworkable theory of the
'just war,' suspends the threat of war over every disfavored nation and makes a
resurrection of international law, not to speak of international peace, exceedingly
difficult, if not impossible." (Pp. 48–9.)

To try to enforce world peace "is a disservice to harmony and a disturber of
the peace." (P. 50.) When aggression is threatened or committed "it is unclear
how the facts are to be determined." (P. 46.) "To attempt to create coercive
machinery . . , whether called collective security or by any other name, is a
technique of war and potential war which impedes the possibility of any useful
co-operation." (P. 54.) It is "not believed that any institutionalized combination
of nations can, by their force or threat of force, except against the weak, reduce
the area of conflict; on the contrary, such an alleged protection against 'aggression' will very likely only enlarge the area and render international relations
hopeless." (P. 56.) Among nations everything must be left to "conciliation . . .
persuasion, and appreciation of self-interest." The "attempt to organize sanctions
has been shocking to intelligent relations and to human welfare" and "a renewed
effort to 'enforce peace' can only result in another debacle." (P. 57.)

velous machines and our ability to control them for social purposes. It is not a subject for academic speculation but a matter of life and death. If we can speed up human organization, both nationally and internationally, the creations of science will give us a life of richness and plenty, such as was never possible before. On the other hand, if we lag behind in governing the uses to which the machines are put, they will mercilessly destroy us in constantly more effective ways and ranges.

This is the problem of our century, and if we fumble it the consequences will not be visited upon some remote generation but upon our own heads and those of our children, not only in death and destruction but through the progressive squandering of our limited mineral resources for destructive purposes.

CHAPTER X

Toward the Future

FOR THE SECOND TIME in twenty-five years we approach the climax of a great world war, a war which should never have been allowed to develop. Again also the American people have made a splendid, successful military effort. We have proved twice that we can go to war and that we can supply to a world coalition the margin of strength essential for victory.

We have proved that we can make war, and during the past fifty years we have demonstrated as conclusively that we cannot make peace. Every citizen of the world knows that. Each newspaperman who travels abroad encounters that knowledge. Every government in the world doubts the ability of the United States to help organize the coming victory, because all know that the Constitution of the United States contains a fatal defect. They know that, so far as constructive effort to build a better world goes, our government is permanently deadlocked within itself by a division of the power to make and execute a foreign policy between the President and the Senate. They must calculate that the constructive plans of the executive are always at the mercy of a self-assertive minority in the Senate.

Most Americans have only begun to comprehend the impact of the Senate's treaty veto upon the other governments and peoples of the world. We have been so accustomed to think of ourselves and our Constitution as the world's chief center of successful, free government that we have not stopped to realize how unreliable we have proved ourselves in the eyes of the world. The other peoples know that we have magnificent impulses but have not been able to make them effective. In 1918 they saw us stand on a high level of world leadership never before attained by any people. Then they watched us become gripped by fratricidal war for two whole years, held helpless in the vise of the treaty veto, until we have been confused, embittered, and removed from world affairs as a constructive force—to drift for twenty years as a mighty and dangerous derelict on an ocean of world anarchy.

It does not help much with the other peoples, either, to tell them that once upon a time long ago the American fathers in their wisdom sat and decided that a tiny fraction of our Congress should have the power to kill or mutilate great multilateral treaties, such as the fathers never even imagined. We have smugly excused ourselves from responsibility by saying that "the other governments knew the Senate minority had this power, didn't they? So they have no complaint."

But that does not go far with the other peoples to excuse us from default and what amounts to breach of faith when everybody's safety and future hangs upon our keeping faith. As Robert N. Wilkin, judge of the United States District Court for Northern Ohio, said recently: "that argument is mere legalistic rationalization," one which would not be accepted in any court of equity. "A corporation which had acquiesced while its president negotiated a contract on terms announced to its directors would not be permitted to escape its obligation on the ground that the contract lacked formal approval by the board of directors as required by the constitution of the company, if in the meantime others had acted on the contract and the contract was in substantial compliance with the previously announced terms."[1]

The peoples of the world cannot be expected to stand longer in respectful awe before an outmoded flaw in our Constitution. What matters to them is the fact that we walked out on them at a crucial turning point in world history and left them to sink or swim in the sea of international anarchy. What matters even more, as another decisive moment approaches, is that we have done nothing about that dangerous flaw in our governmental machinery. Instead of attacking vigorously a source of infection so malignant as to imperil our whole national life, we allowed it to fester and spread through twelve years of malingering and muddling about the World Court. We permitted the "Battalion of Death" to gather recruits and to make the occasion of the small gesture of our recognizing the World Court the vehicle for brewing suspicion and for piling insult upon insult to the forty-eight nations already maintaining the World Court. Year after year we allowed a handful of willful men to defy and frustrate the considered desire and judgment of an overwhelming majority of the American people, including a vast preponderance of the nation's leadership. We permitted the obstructionists to paralyze our decisive hand and influence until the very foundations of human society broke up and dissolved beneath our feet.

A Great Power Which Cannot Make Peace. Now again we have another chance to build institutions of world government strong enough to save us from the final calamity of a third world war, but the noose of the Senate's treaty veto is still around our necks, and there are senators ready to tighten it, a little at a time, as the niceties of scientific reservation-making demand. We all know that a group of senators long opposed the acceptance of our part in this war, and that they will be tempted to rehabilitate themselves by fomenting and riding another wave of blind reaction after it.

In the appendix of his trenchant book, *The American Senate and World Peace*, Kenneth Colegrove gives the voting records of twenty-six senators who on nearly all vital measures voted against the Administration's efforts to stop Hitler. Their names are: *George D. Aiken* (Vermont, Republican), *Hugh A. Butler* (Nebraska, Republican), C. Wayland Brooks (Illinois, Republican), William J. Bulow (South Dakota, Democrat), Arthur Capper (Kansas, Republican), *Bennet Champ Clark* (Missouri, Democrat), D. Worth Clark (Idaho, Democrat), John A. Danaher (Connecticut, Republican), James J. Davis (Pennsylvania, Republican), Rufus C. Holman (Oregon, Republican), *Hiram W. Johnson* (California, Republican), Edwin C. Johnson (Colorado, Democrat), Robert J. La Follette (Wisconsin, Progressive), William Langer (North Dakota, Republican), Pat McCarran (Nevada, Democrat), Gerald P. Nye (North Dakota, Republican), Robert R. Reynolds (North Carolina, Democrat), *Henrik Shipstead* (Minnesota, Republican), *Robert A. Taft* (Ohio, Republican), John Thomas (Idaho, Republican), Charles W. Tobey (New Hampshire, Republican), Arthur H. Vandenberg (Michigan, Republican), David A. Walsh (Massachusetts, Democrat), *Burton K. Wheeler* (Montana, Democrat), *Alexander Wiley* (Wisconsin, Republican) and *Raymond E. Willis* (Indiana, Republican).

Colegrove surveyed the records of these twenty-six senators on eleven vital "stop Hitler" measures and found that only four of the twenty-six voted for as many as two of the eleven bills, while the nine senators whose names are italicized above voted for none of these laws which reversed the disastrous policy of paper-defended isolation.[2]

In September 1944 most of these men were still in the

Senate. Will these senators who were so long and stubbornly wrong in the past be generally reasonable and right in the future? It is possible that they may, but while these senators are numerous enough to strangle any treaty with reservations what government can put any real confidence in the present widespread yearning of the American people for an organized and governed world? It is true that the moral authority of President Roosevelt is world-wide. In the minds of untold millions on every continent he stands as the leader of the present fighting hosts of freedom and democracy. He led their cause before Churchill could, and his application of our great resources has doomed the Axis to defeat. All peoples know that Roosevelt is a liberal statesman who would do his best to build an enduring peace.

But even allowing for these considerations, what does that signify to starved, hopeless peoples and to governments which must cope with world chaos? Woodrow Wilson was also a magnificent leader, the first statesman of truly world stature produced by any nation. He had the confidence of a major or minor fraction of the people of every country. He labored also as valiantly as any man could to turn his promises of a safer world, made with the positive and passive assent of the American people, into reality. He succeeded in making a Covenant of the League of Nations which could have given the world safety. But what happened? His beginning in world government was seized by the Senate and held in a strangling grip until it could be emasculated by deft operations, fourteen in number, and until all the emotions and frustrations stirred in our people by the war could be mobilized into an avalanche of hatred for Wilson's destruction.

That his opponents succeeded every people knows, but not enough Americans understand that in the process the moral sense of the American people was blunted. Shortly before the end came for Wilson he went to St. Louis and spoke these tragic, prophetic words:

"I feel like asking the Secretary of War to get the boys, who went across the water to fight, together on some field where I could go and see them, and I would stand up before them and say: 'Boys, I told you before you went across the seas that this was a war against wars, and I did my best to fulfill the promise, but I am obliged to come to you in mortification and shame and say I have not been able to fulfill the promise. You are betrayed. You fought for something that you did not get.' And the glory of the armies and navies of the United States is gone like a dream in the night, and there ensues upon it, in the suitable darkness of the night, the nightmare of dread which lay upon the nations before this war came; and there will come sometime, in the vengeful providence of God, another struggle in which not a few hundred thousand fine men from America will have to die but as many millions as are necessary to accomplish the final freedom of the peoples of the world."

This poignant appeal was made to a people which had sent its sons to fight in distant lands under the solemn assurance that something was going to be settled, that the enormity of the thing they were asked to squelch would not be permitted soon to happen again. This people had sent its sons, abruptly drawn from factory and field, under the vibrant promise that their sacrifice would end war and really make the world safe for democracy. When Wilson recalled this towering moral obligation to us at St. Louis, on September 6, 1919, his large audience was moved, as were many other audiences on his final gallant tour, but there was no great answering cry from the nation. "When it came to pass," says Judge Wilkin, "that the President of the United States could stand in the center of this nation, confess mortification and shame over his inability to fulfill his promise to its soldier sons, and say to them, 'You are betrayed,' and there was no response, then the spiritual life of the people was indeed at a low ebb."

If such an ebb sets in again after this war there will be determined objectors ready in the Senate to halt all decision until it runs its full devastating course. A distinguished foreign statesman, the president of the Norwegian Storting, Carl Hambro, has already warned us that "the explosive outbursts of personal and political animosity against President Wilson after Versailles will be repeated on a grander scale against President Roosevelt when this war is over. All the atavistic ideas of savage senators in every democratic country, every power of prejudice, every instinct of individual ill will will be marshaled against those who with wisdom and foresight try to build up an orderly international world organization."[3]

Fifty Years of Frustration. This is the picture of instability and undependability which we present to other nations. We can make war, but we cannot make peace. Our efforts to make peace have been nullified in the Senate over and over again. From the moment that we became a world power, as a result of the Spanish-American War, the Senate has frustrated every significant move to substitute the peaceful or international settlement of disputes for war. It rejected the Olney-Pauncefote Arbitration Treaty of 1897 and emasculated the Hay Arbitration Treaties of 1904. It retained a strangle hold on the innocuous Root Arbitration Treaties of 1908–10 and made the Taft Arbitration Treaties of 1911 the occasion for a full-dress rehearsal of the Senate's ability very deliberately to take the life out of an international compact. Then the crowning exhibition of this technique, in 1919–20, upon the greatest treaty ever presented to the Senate was followed by the shameless refinement of all the processes of negation at the expense of the World Court. For twelve years alleged custodians of our safety chiseled away even our meager offer to lend some prestige and support to an international court of law.

Time and again the Senate has reduced us to impotent futility. From the high point of the Taft Arbitration Treaties, which really proposed a substitute for war, the Senate brought us down to the Bryan Treaties of 1913–14, which only sought to postpone conflict a little and never were applied by any nation to do so. Then from the major attempt to forestall future world wars which the League Covenant represented, the Senate reduced us through the futilities of the World Court struggle to the point of persuading the nations to sign the Pact of Paris, a treaty "outlawing" war which was to have no single gun or ship, council or court behind it. Are these cycles of futility never to end?

Once again a supreme world crisis approaches and again the parochial minds of some senators look forward to a grand moment on the stage of history. Again they anticipate that a great treaty, greatest of all, will be laid before the Senate. Again spotlights from every capital in the world will be turned on the floor of the Senate, which will become a great sounding board for "timeless oratory," to be heard, month after month, around the earth. Again bitter, determined men will place themselves in the great treaty's path, never to let it pass. Again clever, scheming politicians, deeply skilled in parliamentary maneuver, will be ready to seize the treaty as a vehicle for personal and political maneuvering—and vengeance. Again the lawyers of the Senate will be posed to treat a great multilateral treaty to the legislative process, just like an Interior Department appropriation bill. Again astute men will frame reservations to kill, and honest men will look at each word until some lack of perfection in the document strikes the eye, the correction of which mushrooms quickly into a compelling mission for the senator.

The stage is set for the greatest senatorial field day of all. But it cannot be allowed to happen. The Senate has had its day as the executioner of our peace treaties. It has been a long day and its fruits have been inexpressibly bitter. This judgment does not mean that our full participation in the attempts of the last four decades to build substitutes for war would have made everything different, or even that this war would have been avoided. It does mean that the Senate would not even permit us to *try* to provide substitutes for war or to make the objectives of the last war stick, in order to save our future from a more horrible fate than the terrible, pitiable catastrophe of 1914–18. This is the offense of the Senate, an offense so calamitous in its effects that we dare not permit it to be repeated. As the censor of our foreign policy the Senate has been fully tried and found wanting. Its frustration of our share in creating and governing an orderly world must be ended. The alternative is a third world war which would cost us half a trillion dollars, exhaust finally the bulk of our mineral resources, and devastate our urban civilization, from one end of this continent to the other. No nation can afford to permit a defect in its government to bankrupt and destroy it.

Four Ways to End the Veto of Our Treaties by One Sixteenth of the Congress

How are the constitutionally ensconced objectors of the Senate to be prevented from frittering away the last remnants of our reputation abroad, and our last chance to save the future of the nation itself? That it must be done is as clear as anything could be. What methods are open to us?

1. *Swift Constitutional Amendment.* The first is the amendment of the Constitution to eliminate the two-thirds vote. This provision was a mistake on the day it was made.

The good intent of the fathers that the Senate and the President should meet as a chummy council on foreign affairs was frustrated at the very start. President George Washington tried to make it work, but the Senate insisted on subjecting his treaty proposals to legislative routine, as it has from that day to this. Washington swore vigorously that he would "never go there again" and he never did. From that day we have been saddled with an unworkable method of conducting foreign affairs. When they were of lesser importance it did not matter much, but as the industrial and technical revolution gathered ever swifter momentum the United States Government appeared ever more frequently to the other nations as a double-headed monster, the senatorial head snatching away what the executive head had conceded in hard-fought treaty bargains, or killing the compact outright.

Never in all human history has any other important people ever subjected itself to an arrangement so plainly and inherently unworkable. After 1789 dozens of new governments were set up. All of their founders examined our Constitution with care and many of them modeled strongly after us, but only Liberia and Guatemala ever copied the two-thirds Senate vote for treaties. Again after the World War many new constitutions were made, but not one of them ever thought it a reasonable thing to give one third of one house of the national legislature a strangle hold on treaties. Yet we remain in our most crucial affairs at the mercy of one sixteenth of our legislators. The vast majority of our people, in Congress and out, can be ready for affirmative action, but it cannot proceed. In his penetrating book, *The Constitution and World Organization*, Professor Edward S. Corwin concludes: "The two-thirds rule was an anomaly before it was ever put into operation, and everything that has happened since 1789, both within the constitutional system and outside of it, has contributed to aggravate its abnormity."[4]

This verdict of a leading authority on constitutional law would be challenged by few of his peers, yet so great is our veneration for old ways that there has been no real revolt against the tyranny of the Senate minorities. The very success of the senatorial censors deadened our perceptions after 1919 and sent us off into "normalcy" when we should have been campaigning incessantly for the end of the treaty veto. All of the energy expended on striving after substitutes for the League of Nations got us nowhere. We are accordingly hard up against the treaty veto again, and the best of all remedies is still its repeal.

Attempts at repeal have been slow to start because of the chilling knowledge that two thirds of the Senate must vote for the submission of any constitutional amendment. This is indeed an appalling hurdle. It gives the hard core of perennial objectors themselves a veto on the repeal of the minority treaty veto. It enables the Senate's own sense of its great importance as the forum for settling the fate of nations to stand in the way of all reform.

Nevertheless the Senate was finally compelled to permit the direct election of senators against its will, and enough popular pressure would relax its grip on our treaties. There is also the distinct possibility that a group of senators may decide to do their country a supreme patriotic service and gain enduring fame for themselves by sponsoring and pushing an amendment to end the veto. There ought to be in the Senate a dozen men, or a half dozen, who can unite behind the realization that the two-thirds vote is a deadly danger to the life of the nation, a mortal danger to the entire Constitution itself, the one thing in it which is working inexorably to bring the whole edifice of American constitutional government down in ruins. Such a group of farsighted senators should be able to see also that from the standpoint even of the Senate's famed clubbiness the treaty veto is a danger to the Senate itself, that the treaty weapon used by a minority on treaties is building a deep distrust in the people for the Senate itself and all its work. The future of the Senate would be far safer if its minorities were relieved of their deadly power. Their excesses are bound to bring the reputation of the whole Senate into deepening disrepute.

There is a unique opportunity here, especially for forward-looking Republican senators, for, after all, it has been mainly Republican senators who have supplied the bulldog obstruction which held us inert during the recent do-nothing decades. Today the game of obstruction is about played out. Those who indulge in it further will bring down upon themselves the wrath of their fellow citizens and of all mankind. Alert senators will see that the applause of the future will come to those who help the world to save itself from the insanity of bigger and better wars—and that Republican senators could not better remove the heavy onus resting upon them than by leading the abolition of the treaty veto. No other move would so convince people that the Republicans could be trusted not to leave us helplessly drifting again toward World War III.

The drift of public opinion is strongly toward amendment of the Constitution. In October 1943 a Gallup poll showed 54 per cent of those interviewed believing that treaties should be approved by an ordinary majority of both houses, while 25 per cent preferred the old two thirds of the Senate rule. In May 1944 another poll was taken, using the same questions, and those favoring reform had increased from 54 per cent to 60 per cent. Those clinging to veto by a minority of the Senate had dropped from 25 per cent to 19 per cent.

This trend may be checked temporarily by the reactionary

provision of the 1944 Republican platform which plumps for two thirds of the Senate rule, not only over treaties but "agreements" as well. This "challenge to common sense," said the Republican New York *Herald Tribune* editorially,[5] "will unquestionably cost the party votes." The consignment of executive "agreements" to the mercies of the two-thirds rule was, said the editor, Senator Robert A. Taft's "own personal and private amendment to the Constitution," one, as we shall see, which senators defending the two-thirds rule are powerless to put into operation, either by custom or by law.

The minority veto of treaties is not capable of successful defense. The more people come to understand that it exists the more they will condemn it. The power of a small band of obstructive senators to veto our decisions in foreign affairs is a power that can be preserved only by failing to use it. Senate minorities can use it once or twice more, perhaps, before they provoke the storm of public wrath that will amend the Constitution, in spite of the Senate's selfish defense of rule by one sixteenth of the Congress.

Indeed, "rule by one sixteenth" puts it charitably, by assuming that all ninety-six senators will vote. But if only a quorum is present, seventeen senators can kill a treaty, and this handful of objectors could represent only 6 per cent of the American people. Some of our most monumental objectors have come from interior states in which few people live.

If the Senate should persist in defending the power of its stubborn minorities to block and disrupt our foreign relations, there is an alternative method of amending the Constitution which has never been used, but can be. If two thirds of the forty-eight state legislatures pass resolutions requesting a constitutional convention to eliminate the Senate's treaty veto the Congress will be compelled to call the convention.

This, too, is a difficult hurdle to surmount, but if the Senate persists in its mutilation of our foreign affairs it can be surmounted. We can have normal popular control of our foreign affairs whenever we become aroused enough to demand it. But it would be far better for the Senate itself to recognize that it cannot defend much longer an indefensible prerogative.

Some senators already recognize the inevitable and welcome it. Senator Claude Pepper of Florida is the author of a proposed amendment to share the scrutiny of treaties with the House of Representatives, by ordinary majorities, and he has supporters. In the House of Representatives several members, including Representative Percy Priest of Tennessee, have sponsored the same amendment and Chairman Sol Bloom, of the House Committee on Foreign Affairs, has published a pamphlet, *Fourteen Points Showing Why the Treaty-Making Power Should Be Shared by the House of Representatives,*[6] which indicts the present undemocratic arrangement bluntly and unanswerably, though of course rebuttal points could be made. It would be strange if the House were not ready to sweep away an archaic rule which denies its members any voice in the decisions which involve the life and death of our youth. No patriotic member of that body should rest content while a handful of senators deliberately whittle away the plans for peace born of ever more frightful wars. It is the Senate and only the Senate which blocks reform.

If the Senate will permit us to vote upon the issue we do not need to be staggered by the normal amount of time required to secure the ratification of a constitutional amendment by the states. On August 19, 1943, the New York *Times* editorially proposed a practical plan for swift elimination of the treaty veto. Our experience in repealing the prohibition amendment showed that an amendment submitted to "conventions" in the states can be ratified in short order. If the Congress would recommend strongly that elections for such conventions be held in all the states on the same day, a decision would not only be obtained quickly, but an additional result of the greatest importance would be achieved; for, says the *Times,* "the vote of the whole people ratifying such an amendment would be itself an immediate notification to the world, stronger even than any congressional resolution, of America's determination this time to assume the great responsibilities which its strength and interests impose upon it."

No more than a few weeks' time would be required to place us in a position to play our part in the coming peace, if the necessary spark of leadership exists in the Congress. This is a time of such urgency that quick thinking and decisive action are imperative. We are entitled to an occasional stroke of statesmanship springing directly from the peoples' representatives, and never more than now.

The Senate should lead the way, but if it does not the House ought to act. There is no reason why the House should submit indefinitely to its exclusion from a voice in treaty making. The House is closer to the people than the Senate and more responsive to them. It does not suffer so much from the sense of omnipotence which comes to so many senators. In the event of continued recalcitrance in the Senate the House would do well to send a proposed constitutional amendment on treaty making up to the Senate by an overwhelming vote, one which would prove to the people that neither political party is going to play politics with the future of the nation this time. Here is a rare opportunity for the leadership of either party to distinguish itself.

2. *An Advance Pledge by the Senate to Support Strong, Effective Organization of the Peace.* Fortunately there is evidence that in the Senate itself there is keen awareness of the extent to which its past actions have prejudiced the

future. Four of the younger senators have given proof that they knew the making of the peace could not begin until the Senate had given convincing assurance of a change of conduct.

On March 16, 1943, Senators Joseph H. Ball of Minnesota and Harold H. Burton of Ohio (Republicans) united with Senators Lister Hill of Alabama and Carl Hatch of New Mexico (Democrats) to submit to the Senate the following resolution:

Resolved, That the Senate advises that the United States take the initiative in calling meetings of representatives of the United Nations for the purpose of forming an organization of the United Nations with specific and limited authority:

(1) To assist in co-ordinating and fully utilizing the military and economic resources of all member nations in the prosecution of the war against the Axis.

(2) To establish temporary administrations for Axis-controlled areas of the world as these are occupied by United Nations forces, until such time as permanent governments can be established.

(3) To administer relief and assistance in economic rehabilitation in territories of member nations needing such aid and in Axis territory occupied by United Nations forces.

(4) To establish procedures and machinery for peaceful settlement of disputes and disagreements between nations.

(5) To provide for the assembly and maintenance of a United Nations military force and to suppress by immediate use of such force any future attempt at military aggression by any nation.

That the Senate further advises that any establishment of such United Nations organization provide machinery for its modification, for the delegation of additional specific and limited functions to such organization, and for admission of other nations to membership, and that member nations should commit themselves to seek no territorial aggrandizement.

This resolution was at once attacked as being too detailed, and as going too far. A first poll of the Senate showed the necessary thirty-two senators to be opposed to some part of it. There was particular objection to Point 5, calling for an international police force. Of course there would be, for that is a pledge of international government with teeth in it, one really strong enough to keep the peace. No senator who voted for that could thereafter whittle away a United Nations constitution with much aplomb. His constituents would become acutely aware of him. Hence the ex-isolationists were averse to a resolution with such clear and definite points in it.

In March 1943 a subcommittee of the Senate Foreign Relations Committee was appointed to consider the Ball resolution and a number of others, but nothing happened for many weeks. Confronted with the massive inertia of the Senate Committee, the House Committee on Foreign Relations unanimously adopted, on September 21, 1943, a resolution by Representative J. W. Fulbright of Arkansas which said:

Resolved by the House of Representatives (the Senate concurring), that the Congress hereby expresses itself as favoring the creation of appropriate international machinery with power adequate to establish and to maintain a just and lasting peace, among the nations of the world, and as favoring participation by the United States therein, through its constitutional processes.

Naturally the Senate was reluctant to promise not to sabotage the peace again. After a two-month summer recess there were many reports that the Senate couldn't act until it knew more about what Russia and Britain intended. When Senator Nye voiced this feeling, on September 25, the Associated Press quoted him as summing up the attitude of the majority of the Senate.

The adoption of the Fulbright resolution in the House by a majority of 360 to 29 seemed only to strengthen the Senate's aversion to pledging its future good behavior. Senator Gillett reported, on September 23, that there was some feeling in the Senate that the House had gone out of bounds. The next day Chairman Connally issued a statement in which he said that his Committee did not desire "at this particular moment to afford opportunity for intemperate and trouble-making debate on the floor of the Senate." An "ill-considered debate" might "produce irritations or vexations at a critical period in the prosecution of the war."

At this juncture the Administration, which had been keeping in the background, let it be known that a debate was not to be feared and that a postwar policy resolution adopted by the Senate would greatly strengthen Secretary Hull's hands in the Moscow Conference. Dispatches from London also indicated uneasiness over the inability of the Senate even to discuss postwar policy. The New York *Times* observed, on September 23, that in this important matter "the Senate Committee has had its chance and muffed it. Twenty-five weeks have passed since it created a subcommittee to write a resolution of this kind. For twenty-five weeks, when the world was waiting to hear the voice of Congress, that subcommittee never peeped," and on September 26 the New York *Herald Tribune* spoke of the Senate as being "in a fit of collective sulks." Senator Ball also suggested that it might become necessary to move that the Committee be discharged from the consideration of postwar policy.

These pressures led the Senate subcommittee to decide to act, on the twenty-ninth, and on October 14 it reported the following resolution, by a vote of 7 to 1, Senator La Follette dissenting:

Resolved by the Senate of the United States: that the war against all our enemies be waged until complete victory is achieved;

That the United States, acting through its constitutional processes, join with free and sovereign nations in the establishment and maintenance of international authority with power to prevent aggression and to preserve the peace of the world.

In an effort to stiffen the resolution Senator Claude Pepper of Florida offered as a substitute for the last paragraph of the Connally resolution this proposal:

That the United States, acting through its constitutional processes, join with the other United Nations and such free and sovereign nations as may be duly admitted, in the establishment and maintenance of an international organization to promote cooperation among nations, with authority to settle international disputes peacefully, and with power, including military force, to suppress military aggression and to preserve the peace of the world.

Pepper led a group of fourteen senators who joined in sponsoring his amendment. Besides Senator Pepper the group included: Senators Joseph Ball (Republican, Minnesota), Harold H. Burton (Republican, Ohio), Carl A. Hatch (Democrat, New Mexico), Lister Hill (Democrat, Alabama), Styles Bridges (Republican, New Hampshire), Sheridan Downey (Democrat, California), Burnet R. Maybank (Democrat, South Carolina), Joseph F. Guffey (Democrat, Pennsylvania), Theodore F. Green (Democrat, Rhode Island), James E. Murray (Democrat, Montana), Harry S. Truman (Democrat, Missouri), Harley Kilgore (Democrat, West Virginia), and Homer Ferguson (Republican, Michigan).

This new group of fighters for an organized peace pressed strongly for their statement but without making any appreciable headway until the Moscow Conference went on record for a United Nations organization. Then the two following paragraphs were accepted by the Committee, on November 3, and by the Senate on November 5:

(Resolved) That the Senate recognizes the necessity of there being established at the earliest practicable date a general international organization, based on the principle of the sovereign equality of all peace-loving states, and open to membership by all such states, large and small, for the maintenance of international peace and security.

That, pursuant to the Constitution of the United States, any treaty made to effect the purposes of the resolution, on behalf of the Government of the United States with any other nation or any association of nations, shall be made only by and with the advice and consent of the Senate of the United States, provided two thirds of the senators present concur.

Thus amended, the Connally resolution was accepted by the Senate on November 5 by a vote of 85 to 5. The opposition votes came from Senators Johnson (Republican, California), Langer (Republican, North Dakota), Reynolds (Democrat, North Carolina), Shipstead (Republican, Minnesota), and Wheeler (Democrat, Montana). Senator La Follette, absent, would have voted no. If absentees had been present the vote would have been 90 to 6.

The gains from this resolution are striking. There is assurance that we will not make another separate peace with Germany and that we will take part in a new or revived League of Nations. Quite clearly the Senate has arrived at 1919. It will accept "Wilson's League," but strongly implies that it will not go beyond it. But is a league such as might have worked after 1918 sufficient for 1943? As the air age bursts upon us with its frightful and incalculable power, will a loose confederation of nations be able to harness and control it?

A second reading of the Connally resolution also brings out the inevitable reservations, two all-sufficient ones. The resolution twice refers to national sovereignty as the base upon which we must build. Yet there is no way by which absolute national sovereignty can be reconciled with "international authority with power adequate to prevent aggression." One principle or the other must prevail, and under the terms of both the Senate and the Moscow resolutions senators can adamantly refuse to accept any organs of international government on the ground that our "sovereignty" is compromised. The sovereignty loophole is big enough to fly a cloud of great bombers through, on their way to destroy the cities of this continent. Professor Corwin has compressed the whole commotion about national sovereignty into one sentence: *"When Total War is the price of Total Sovereignty, the price is too high."*[7]

The Senate's double insistence on everything being approved by a two-thirds vote of the Senate is also ominous for the future. It is said that the purpose of this reservation was to prevent the President from assuming that everything was now settled and compel him to bring the coming peace settlements before the Senate. If so, the two-thirds vote prescription invites every lukewarm supporter of the principle of international organization to demand reservations to the key articles of the United Nations constitution, on penalty of having his vote kill two votes for the treaty. In effect the Senate offers to accept the League of Nations—1919 model—in exchange for retaining its strangle hold on treaties. If this is not true, let the ninety senators who approved the Connally resolution send a constitutional amendment to the people ending forever the power of one third of their number to emasculate the great treaties we must have to live in a blitzkrieg world. Such an amendment springing from the Senate would be ratified in record time, amid resounding applause and great national relief. It would give present senators a permanent niche in our history as the men big enough to remove a great danger from the national life by diminishing one of the Senate's own "prerogatives." The Senate will not protect its own reputation and future by clinging to the right of its minorities to emasculate our international compacts.

We have no assurance that the present chastened mood of senators will last. In the absence of action on their part to remove the menace of the minority veto from our future the Connally resolution will stand as a promise that the Senate will not, or may not, kill the coming attempt at organizing peace in exchange for retaining the oppressive power to veto treaties by the action of a third of the Senators present. The intent to preserve the tyranny of the two-thirds vote is further evidenced by the refusal of the Senate to join in the Fulbright resolution or to permit the House to accept its own formula. Though the House forced the Senate to act, the Senate will not admit the right of the House to any share in fixing our foreign policy.

The Senate has moved far, but if it stops where it is it will be standing firmly upon the right of all Senate objectors to raise the shibboleths of national sovereignty and mobilize a third of the senators against the organization of the peace. As matters stand the kickers are to have full scope against the last chance we shall ever have to get a workable international government, for if we miss this one the full hideousness of modern war will come home to us on this continent in the next world war.

3. *The Approval of All Controversial International Agreements by Congressional Joint Resolutions.* Yet a third method of breaking the Senate bottleneck is readily open to us. Our constitutional history includes a long record of important adjustments of our foreign relations by joint resolutions of Congress, requiring only majority votes. In 1844 the Senate blocked a treaty for the annexation of Texas by a vote more than two to one, but after the annexationists won the next election Texas was annexed by a joint resolution in 1845. Again, in 1897, the opposition in the Senate delayed the annexation of Hawaii by treaty for a year, when it was accomplished by joint resolution.

Even more significantly, the United States accepted membership in the International Labor Organization by joint resolution, on June 19, 1934. This organization bears the same organic relation to the League of Nations that the World Court does, but there was no last-ditch fight against it, as there would probably have been had adherence to it been presented as a treaty. The Hull trade agreements have also been authorized and validated three times by the Congress, at three-year intervals, *in advance of* their negotiation, by simple joint resolutions. The tariff-making power, one of the greatest, most prized, and most explosive powers possessed by the Congress, has been placed in the hands of the executive, to be exercised in a careful, orderly manner, and everyone has scrupulously avoided calling the trade agreements "treaties." This is an extremely important development, but it does not constitute a more complete reversal of national policy than the Lend-Lease agreements. These reverse the impractical war-debt policy of the last war and will have profound effects upon the entire field of our international relations. Yet they are all authorized by the method of joint resolution.

If no one is willing to face a struggle with the Senate to amend the Constitution, this method of avoiding the treaty veto is wide open to the Congress. It can approve all controversial treaties by joint resolution, avoiding the use of the word "treaty." There is the disadvantage, not a crucial one, that the Constitution is amended by usage, instead of by a single act of the national will, and there is the possibility that the courts might someday look hard at the letter of the Constitution and invalidate some international action not authorized by "treaty." It is not likely, however, that any foreseeable Supreme Court majority would wish to assume the obstructionist or perfectionist mantle of Senate minorities, and to block the absolutely essential conduct of our international business. If the Senate persists in blocking the amendment of the Constitution to end the power of its minorities over treaties the Constitution will be amended by usage, with increasing rapidity.

The strong probability that the treaties following this war will be approved by joint resolutions was indicated by a formal statement issued by Senator Vandenberg on August 17, 1943, after a long conference with Senator Theodore F. Green, Democrat, of Rhode Island, and two high officials of the State Department. The statement follows:

We are making excellent progress toward an agreement which rewrites the objectionable clauses in the original draft [of the relief and rehabilitation pact] and toward simplified procedure for submitting these obligations to Congress for approval.

I am hopeful that this mutual effort may be sufficiently successful to set a pattern for other postwar problems short of the actual treaty of final peace. It ought to be possible for reasonable men to find a formula which will permit the merits of these many unavoidable war liquidations to be considered without detouring primarily into procedural rows. It ought to be possible to satisfy the constitutional process and still expedite essential results.

Continuing its report, on August 18, the New York *Times* stated that Secretary Hull had long held out for making the postwar settlements through a series of executive agreements, without any reference to the Senate. This led to a clash with Senator Tom Connally of Texas, chairman of the Foreign Relations Committee, which nearly broke up the conferences on the subject. Others intervened and there had apparently been worked out "the most significant accomplishment in the field of foreign relations for a generation." This would indeed be true if, as reported, Senator Vandenberg was "speaking for at least a majority of Senate Republicans."

An agreement to approve the international agreements

arising from this war by joint resolutions should be highly acceptable to the majority of Republican senators, since it would free them from the fatal temptation to use the one-third treaty veto as a weapon against the postwar treaties. The catastrophic effects of another deadlock of that kind would fall inescapably upon the political party responsible, as well as upon the nation.

It is true that Vandenberg made an exception of the final treaty of peace, and this could be important. On the other hand, all groups studying postwar problems, and most individual students, have agreed that there should be this time no grand peace conference, on the traditional model, with a stupendous treaty resulting. Instead there is general agreement that the many and varied problems of saving the conquered lands from complete collapse and restoring them to health, of policing the enemy and building permanent world organization, should be the subject of many separate international conferences, each producing its own legislation. The reasons for this policy are cogently inherent in the present situation, but underlying them all is the necessity of withholding from the United States Senate another world platform, upon which the long-formed habits of its constitutional objectors and perfectionists would irresistibly assert themselves.

The prolonged and agonizing dissection of the world's hopes in the Senate cannot be permitted to happen again. The Senate is, after all, only one house of the legislature of one nation among many. It is entitled to some voice in building the new world, if it will try to build instead of destroy, but not to sit as a final court of last resort upon the fate of all humanity.

4. *The Conduct of Our Foreign Affairs through Executive Agreements.* If this realization is at last penetrating the Senate itself, it may not be necessary finally to resort to the

fourth and last method open to us to get the world's work performed—the method of executive agreements, supported only by such enabling legislation as Congress sees fit to enact.

The conduct of a nation's foreign relations, including the making of treaties, has always and everywhere been an executive function. The admission of our Senate to a role in treaty making was an experiment dictated by unusual conditions. As a move in the direction of democracy it was a step in the right direction, but the arming of a small minority with the power of negation was a cardinal error, an undemocratic arrangement. Even our Constitution, however, leaves the main power to control foreign relations in the hands of the executive.

By the very nature of things, also, it must remain there. It is inherently an executive function. International action to promote and defend the interests of the nation is perpetually required. It must go on constantly and only the executive can direct it. A legislative body may be consulted, if its appropriate organs are not irreconcilably opposed to the executive, but it cannot direct foreign policy. The legislature may properly have a broad right of veto over treaties, if it is exercised in the large, but it can properly decide only whether, on the whole, the proposed agreement is a good thing.

In pursuance of the President's inherent executive power, our executive has made executive agreements having the same effect as treaties, from the beginning of the Republic. In his exhaustive study, *International Executive Agreements*, Wallace McClure has documented this record through several chapters to the conclusion that an executive agreement not in contravention of any provision of the Constitution and not in conflict with any act of Congress is binding on all the executive and law-enforcing agencies of the government "and is the equivalent of law." Then, after weighing the constitutional history involved through five additional chapters, he holds that the Congress can by simple majorities "legally accomplish under the Constitution anything that can be legally accomplished by the treaty-making power as specifically defined in the Constitution." McClure believes this conclusion fortified by "the Supreme Court's positive and unequivocal interpretation of the Constitution" and he holds that "whenever controversial questions are involved the Senate method of treaty making can quietly be abandoned, leaving routine treaties to be handled by the Senate alone."[8]

This easiest solution of our major constitutional problem implies that where appropriations or other implementing action of Congress are necessary the Congress will co-operate. When Congress is at war with the executive this assumption may not hold. At other times the Congress, or either branch of it, could take the responsibility of nullifying an executive agreement. But that risk is much smaller than the danger of veto or emasculation by thirty-three senators. And if this method of getting things done looks like executive usurpation to senators they can readily reduce its use by consenting to a constitutional amendment which will permit treaty making with the consent of an ordinary majority of both houses of Congress.[9]

Under the compulsions of the air age, also, it will be less and less feasible for any part of Congress to frustrate the transaction of international business. As McClure points out, "do-nothing-ism cannot even be counted on to preserve the status quo, which, if endangered, may require prompt, vigorous action." In the coming century both the Senate and the Congress will be absolutely compelled to forsake "the negative merit of not doing harm" for "the positive merit of doing good."[10]

Which of the four methods for eliminating the Senate's

treaty veto will be used? The first suggested, swift constitutional amendment, would clear the air most quickly, giving decisive evidence that we do not mean to let negation frustrate the peace again. Yet a combination of the other three methods, all constitutional, can be effective. By one device or another the Senate bottleneck will be broken. The Senate has had full opportunity to help build a safer and better world, and throughout the whole period since we became a world power—up to November 1943—it has on all the decisive occasions chosen to obstruct. But obstruction cannot continue much longer. If the Senate's minority veto is not eliminated it will be by-passed. The life of this nation must go on, and the urgent business of building a world society proceed.

THE SENATE CANNOT ATTACH RESERVATIONS AND AMENDMENTS TO GREAT MULTILATERAL TREATIES

The end of the minority veto will not, however, remove all danger of national frustration in the Senate. The deadly habit of fighting treaties by amendments and reservations, or of honestly trying to perfect them for the United States by the same means, will long persist. It has reached the status of a deep-seated senatorial disease. It is bound up with the habits of lawyers and with the legislative process itself. Yet a great multilateral treaty, the result of long and close negotiation, cannot be changed by any legislature as if it had originated in one of its own committees. Such a treaty is the result of much give and take by the representatives of many "sovereign" powers. It has to remain acceptable to the other parties. It cannot be altered by any parliament unless all have the same right, and that leads to manifest futility. If one legislature can change the treaty, so can those of the other thirty United Nations. If we can change the conditions agreed upon, then the others have a right to consider these changes and propose counterchanges—the very process which bogged us down in the case of the World Court, and would have done so had the Senate's reservations to the League Covenant been sent abroad.

The business of "perfecting" a great multilateral treaty to suit the whims of national legislators is a game at which only one parliament can play. When others join in there is plainly renegotiation and recrimination to the end of time. Our Senate has appeared to establish a right to tinker with any and all treaties by long usage only because our foreign relations were a relative luxury, not a daily necessity of our very existence, and because the easier conditions of the nineteenth century permitted the other governments to humor the Senate, usually reluctantly and sometimes angrily.

Today the time when that can be done is gone. There are too many desperate problems to be settled. The Senate can still weigh the advantages and disadvantages of each international compact in the large, deciding whether, on the whole, it is a good thing for the United States, but it cannot dot the *i*s, cross the *t*s, and embalm its fears in a miscellaneous assortment of reservations. The other governments cannot and will not longer permit the Senate that luxury. They cannot afford to allow the United States Senate to continue to act as a death house for treaties which affect the peace or determine the fate of all. Nor can we.

WE ARE RESPONSIBLE FOR THE SENATE

It is true that the habits of the Senate are old and deep-seated. They are not likely to change of themselves, even under the impact of this incredible Second World War, unless the American people who create the senators maintain responsibility for them. If enough senators get out their treaty scalpels, only a real rising among their constituents can save us from another era of frustration, ending in a still worse period of death and devastation. Unless there is deep awareness in our people that tinkering with treaties kills them, they will be tinkered with again, even under ordinary majority rule.

Senators have, after all, played fast and loose with treaty making because we allowed them to do so. The Senate became a veritable citadel of isolationism after 1935 because most of us were seeking cellars. Our people knew in 1918 and 1919 what should be done, but not enough of them insisted on its being done. Once again, too, the result will depend upon our constancy and determination, for unless we remain vigilantly alert, all sorts of senatorial quirks and phobias will again confuse and divide and weary us.

We shall lose the peace again, unless we fight and work until it is won. We shall fail to win it, unless we are fully resolved not to take no as an answer this time from any set of isolationist or "nationalist" politicians. The final responsibility is on us. It may be that we cannot really learn what kind of world we live in until hostile bombers and robot bombs are overhead, but we ought not to require that last instruction.

Toward World Government

We do not know what the full outlines of the coming world order will be, but we know that it must come, since life is no longer tolerable without it. If this war has done nothing else it has shattered the myth of national sovereignty. Within the past ten years not one of the Great Powers has been able to defend its soil from devastating attack. We have escaped the easiest. Britain is coming off next best, but only because the two greatest of world powers came to her relief.

The horrible fate of China, and of France, is known to all, yet Russia's suffering has been second to none. No one of the three aggressor regimes dared to stand alone; they banded themselves together and will all end the war with their cities in ruins, their best manhood gone, their lands truly impoverished. We should not be deceived either by our relative immunity to present attack, for we dared not stand on our own feet and wait until all friends were gone.

In these deadly years the alert citizens of every nation have discovered that the nation is not enough, that to live tolerably they must have something more—a higher level of protection, to which they must yield a fraction of their sovereignty in order to keep the bulk of it, the precious essentials of ordinary self-government. Thus the United Nations is not something imposed on us, but something we seek and are glad to give loyalty to, a loyalty which will deepen and dignify our national patriotism, much as the latter makes fruitful and productive our local patriotisms. We add a level of government to preserve all the others, not to weaken or destroy them.

No Anglo-Saxon needs to be told that federation strengthens, and it should be apparent to all that a federation of the nations with real powers is now demanded, to replace the League of Nations, that weak confederation of nations which aroused so many extravagant fears a little while ago. That the federation of the future will build on the experience of the League of Nations is as much to be expected.

The extent of its powers is naturally the subject of much debate, but everyone assumes that the existing World Court will be the top judicial organ of the United Nations. All plans agree on that point. No voice is raised against the Permanent Court of International Justice, and no one need doubt the fulfillment of the prediction of Attorney General Homer H. Cummings in 1934 that "in the fullness of time the World Court is destined to become the most useful, the most majestic tribunal in all the history of the human race."[11]

If the reader believes the confidence in a sane, effective world organization of the United Nations expressed above is premature, he can help to make it so: (1) by putting his faith in an "American Century" of world policing by the United States; (2) by relying on alliance with one or two strong states, inviting a final balance-of-power clash; (3) by encouraging or failing to resist the idea that we cannot co-operate with Soviet Russia in a collective world order; (4) by relapsing into simple inertia or succumbing to the allurements of a new "normalcy."

A strong, working organization of the nations can be postponed again, until after a third world war—if there is then anything left to organize.

Notes

CHAPTER I

[1] James Brown Scott, editor, *Instructions to the American Delegates to The Hague Peace Conferences and Their Official Reports* (New York, 1916), p. 9.

[2] Raymond B. Fosdick, "A Way of Escape from War," *International Conciliation* (February 1932), No. 277, p. 60.

[3] Charles Warren, "The Supreme and the World Court 1832–1932," *International Conciliation* (April 1933), No. 289, pp. 20–21.

This success of the Court did not, however, remove the forebodings of great contemporaries about the future. Chief Justice Marshall wrote to Justice Story, in 1832: "I yield slowly and reluctantly to the conclusion that our constitution cannot last"; and in 1837 Ralph Waldo Emerson inscribed in his *Journal*: "Society has played out its last stroke. It is checkmated. . . . The present generation is as bankrupt of principles and hope as of property." (Pp. 9–10.)

[4] William Ladd, *An Essay on a Congress of Nations* (Reprinted from the original edition of 1840, New York, 1916), p. 34.

[5] Scott, op. cit., pp. 9–10.

[6] *Senate Documents*, Vol. 14, 66th Congress, 1st Session, pp. 262–79.

[7] Scott, op. cit., Annex B, pp. 14–16; David Jayne Hill, *The Problem of a World Court* (New York, 1927), pp. 10–14. The instructions were drafted by Dr. Hill as Assistant Secretary of State.

[8] Manley O. Hudson, *The Permanent Court of International Justice, 1920–42* (New York, 1943), pp. 3–36. This monumental book by a judge of the World Court is the outstanding authority on its antecedents, origins, and operation.

[9] Hill, op. cit., p. 17.

[10] Scott, op. cit., pp. 72–77, 129–32.

[11]*Selections from the Correspondence of Theodore Roosevelt and Henry Cabot Lodge* (New York, 1925), Vol. II, p. 111. After the defeat of the Hay-Pauncefote Arbitration Treaty in 1897 the *Nation* said, on December 20, 1900: "We have been trying to conclude important international agreements during the past fifteen years, but have seen one after another of them go to wreck in the Senate. . . . In a newly hatched and loudly cackling 'world power,' the inability to make a treaty is little short of ludicrous."

About the same time A. Maurice Low concluded that a treaty was always sure to meet political opposition, "or opposition originating in prejudice, self-interest, or ignorance." A. Maurice Low, "The Oligarchy of the Senate," *North American Review* (February 1902), Vol. 174, p. 241.

[12]Ibid., p. 404.

[13]On July 21, 1919, when the Covenant of the League of Nations was before the Senate, Senator Lodge was visited by Mr. James G. McDonald, chairman of the League of Free Nations Association, and Mr. Allen T. Burns, president of the National Conference of Social Work, in behalf of the treaty. Mr. Burns's account of the interview is as follows: "In our discussion of the treaty situation with Senator Lodge he summarized his attitude and purpose in the following manner: taking from the shelves of the foreign relations committee room a copy of the general arbitration treaty with Great Britain negotiated by President Taft in 1911, the chairman pointed out the amendments and reservations made by the Senate. Exultingly he remarked: 'And President Taft never saw fit to return the treaty to Great Britain. We shall deal with the Versailles Treaty in the same way. If President Wilson does not see fit to return it to our Allies, that is his responsibility.' Then with a snap of his jaw and a bang of his fist, 'That is the way to handle such treaties!'" The Springfield *Republican,* October 31, 1920. Previously published in the New York *Evening Post* after careful consideration by its editor, Edwin F. Gay. Verified by an interview with Mr. Burns on August 26, 1931.

[14]From the introduction to *The World Court,* by A. S. Bustamante (New York, 1925), p. IX. An influential organization, the Lake Mohonk Society, was organized in 1895 for the sole purpose of propagandizing the judicial settlement of international disputes. See the volume of *Mohonk Addresses* (Boston, 1910), by E. E. Hale and David J. Brewer, covering the years 1895–1908.

CHAPTER II

[1]J. W. Wheeler-Bennett and Maurice Fanshawe, *Information on the World Court, 1918–28* (London, 1929), pp. 147–53.

[2]Theodore Roosevelt, *America and the World War* (New York, 1915), pp. 78–9; the *Independent* (January 4, 1915), Vol. 81, p. 13.

[3]The momentous events so briefly sketched here have been recorded in detail in my *The United States and the League of Nations, 1918–20* (New York, 1932). An absorbing history, *The League to Enforce Peace*, by Ruhl J. Bartlett, was published by the University of North Carolina Press in 1944.

[4]*Enforced Peace* (New York, 1916), p. 10. Powerful movements of the same character mobilized opinion in Britain, Holland, and other countries.

[5]For accounts of this conference see New York *Times*, October 29 and 30, 1920; Corinne Roosevelt Robinson, *My Brother, Theodore Roosevelt* (New York, 1921), pp. 361–62; Fleming, op. cit., pp. 72–76.

[6]D. F. Fleming, *The United States and World Organization, 1920–33*, p. 24.

[7]Chapel Hill, 1944, p. 130.

[8]George Harvey, *Henry Clay Frick the Man* (New York, 1928), pp. 329–30.

[9]Lodge wrote that he "felt convinced that President Wilson would prevent the acceptance of the treaty with reservations if he possibly could. I based this opinion on the knowledge I had acquired as to Mr. Wilson's temperament, intentions and purposes . . . when a correct analysis of Mr. Wilson's probable attitude was an element of vital moment to me in trying to solve the intricate problem which I and those with whom I acted were compelled to face." H. C. Lodge, *The Senate and the League of Nations* (New York, 1925), pp. 218–19, 289.

[10]*Literary Digest*, November 29, 1919.

[11]Lodge, op. cit., pp. 147–48; Harvey, op. cit., p. 325.

[12]Lodge, op. cit., p. 194. Describing the tactics of the irreconcilables, Lodge once said plaintively that they addressed him in language which "no man of my age should be obliged to hear." Mark Sullivan, "America and the League: Six Years After," *World's Work* (January 1926), Vol. 51, p. 291.

[13]New York *Times*, New York *Tribune*, June 11, 1920; James E. Watson, *As I Knew Them* (Indianapolis, 1936), pp. 215–16.

[14]C. H. Rowell, "The Foreign Policy of the United States since the War," *The Problems of Peace* (Oxford, 1927), p. 177. These public performances were supplemented with equally reassuring private statements by Harding to both sides.

[15]Besides Charles E. Hughes, Elihu Root, Herbert Hoover, and Henry L. Stimson, the thirty-one included: Henry W. Taft, Oscar S. Straus, George W. Wickersham, William Allen White, Lyman Abbott, Paul D. Cravath, Nicholas Murray Butler, and twelve other prominent university and college presidents.

Chapter III

[1] Philip C. Jessup, *Elihu Root* (New York, 1938), Vol. II, p. 418.

[2] *Procès Verbaux of the Proceedings of the Commission*, 5th Meeting, pp. 133–35, 138–39, Annex No. 2.

[3] *Records of the Second Assembly, Plenary Meetings*, pp. 236–37, 246–49, 281.

[4] Hudson, *The Permanent Court of International Justice, 1920–42*, p. 127.

[5] Fleming, *The United States and World Organization, 1920–33*, pp. 63–72. The New York *Times*, April 21, 1926, called Secretary Hughes's notes to the League in this period "models of frigidity."

[6] New York *Times*, July 15 and 20, 1922, October 19, 1924.

[7] Edward A. Harriman, *The Constitution at the Cross Roads* (New York, 1925), pp. 135–41. The author wrote as a member of the District of Columbia bar.

[8] *League of Nations Official Journal*, November–December 1920, p. 15.

[9] New York *Times*, March 20, 1923.

[10] Ibid., July 1, 1923.

[11] Ibid., December 14, 1923.

[12] *Congressional Record*, Vol. 65, Pt. 6, p. 5554; New York *Times*, April 28, May 1, 1924.

[13] *Literary Digest*, Vol. 81, May 24, 1924, p. 13.

[14] See the New York *Times* from April 1923 to January 1926, especially the issues of March 4, October 18, and December 13, 1925.

[15] Ibid., April 12, 1923.

[16] Soon after Mr. Hoover's statement two books were published to warn Americans against the dangers of entanglement through the World Court. *The World Court Myth*, by James V. Giblin and Arthur L. Brown (Wright and Potter, Boston, 1926), is an "America first" argument. Objecting to the advisory-opinion function and maintaining that in several cases the Court's opinion had not been enforced by the Council, the book concludes that the Court is "not a court at all, but a *limited panel of supplemental diplomacy*, for it was suggested, authorized and created through the League of Nations." There was "no need whatsoever of joining any world court" for none of our major foreign policies or problems

(enumerated) would be "submitted for foreign determination." The old methods were sufficient and "the will for peace in the past, at present and in the future is a guarantee that any matters which are in the least justiciable will be fairly and equitably handled through present available means of adjustment." (Pp. 380–81.)

The United States Senate and the World Court, by Frances Kellor and Antonia Hatvany (Thomas Seltzer, New York, 1925), ended with two chapters calling for strong stiffening of the Harding-Hughes reservations in all directions, in order to enable the Republican party to fulfill its contradictory pledges to adhere to the Court and to "assume no obligations under the Covenant." This dilemma was to be avoided by refusing to have anything to do with the administration of the Court, including the election of judges. To avoid the administrative contamination involved in paying a share of the Court's expenses through the League treasury, it was proposed that we recognize the Court only after it had been made fiscally autonomous, so that it could decide what we should pay and send us a statement direct. Other proposed reservations provided extensively for protection against advisory opinions and for the consummation of the outlawry of war. (Pp. 241–57.)

Chapter IV

[1] New York *Times*, December 6, 1925.

[2] From an address by Charles E. Hughes to the American Society of International Law on April 27, 1923. Published by the Chamber of Commerce of the United States. In that speech Hughes demanded to know "In what are we entangled? Are we to abandon the effort to dispose of international controversies by judicial settlement, which has been a feature of American policy since the foundation of the government?" (P. 19.)

[3] Manley O. Hudson, in an address to the National Council for the Prevention of War, Washington, October 30, 1929.

[4] Moore's memorandum was printed in the *Congressional Record* (January 4, 1926), pp. 1027–31. See also Leland M. Goodrich, "The Nature of the Advisory Opinions of the Permanent Court of International Justice," *American Journal of International Law* (1932), p. 740; P.C.I.J. Series D., No. 2, pp. 383–98.

[5] *Congressional Record*, Vol. 67, Pt. 2, pp. 1236–45.

[6] Quoted from D. F. Fleming, *The Treaty Veto of the American Senate*, p. 194.

[7] *Congressional Record*, Vol. 67, Pt. 2, p. 1497.

[8] Ibid., p. 2037.

[9]Ibid., p. 2191.

[10]Ibid., pp. 1971–72.

[11]Ibid., pp. 2293–94.

[12]New York *Times*, January 28, 1926; *United States Daily*, September 24, 1926; *Congressional Record*, Vol. 67, Pt. 3, pp. 2556–57.

[13]See the beginning of Chapter II.

CHAPTER V

[1]*League of Nations, Official Journal* (April 1926, 7th year), No. 4, p. 536.

[2]New York *Times*, March 19 and 20, 1926.

[3]Ibid., April 3, 4, 1926.

[4]*World Peace Foundation Pamphlets* (1926), Vol. IX, No. 8, p. 622.

[5]*United States Daily*, December 31, 1927.

[6]E. E. Lape, "A Way Out of the Court Deadlock," *Atlantic Monthly* (October 1927), Vol. 140, p. 529.

[7]*Publication de la Société des Nations*, V. Questions Juridiques (1926), Vol. 24, p. 6. See also Vol. 25, pp. 3, 7.

[8]New York *Tribune*, September 24, 1926.

[9]Kansas City *Star*, November 12, 1926.

CHAPTER VI

[1]New York *Times*, March 11, 1928.

[2]*United States Daily*, February 20, 1929.

[3]John E. Stoner, S. O. *Levinson and the Pact of Paris* (Chicago, 1943), p. 167. See also p. 78.

[4]New York *Times*, March 7, 1929.

[5]Ibid., March 12, 1929.

[6]Hudson, *The Permanent Court of International Justice, 1920–42*, pp. 224–25, 236.

[7]*Current History* (May 1929), Vol. XXX, No. 2, p. 312.

[8]Hudson, op. cit., pp. 225–33.

[9]George H. Haynes, *The Senate of the United States* (Boston, 1938), Vol. II, p. 711.

CHAPTER VII

[1]Hudson, *Progress in International Organization* (Stanford, 1932), p. 67.

[2]Dennison, op. cit., p. 128.

[3]Edwin M. Borchard, "The Customs Union Advisory Opinion," *American Journal of International Law* (October 1931), Vol. 25, pp. 711–16.

[4]*American Journal of International Law* (1932), Vol. 26, p. 109.

[5]John W. Davis, "The World Court Settles the Question," *International Conciliation* (February 1932), No. 277, pp. 70, 71, 78.

[6]C. Grove Haines and Ross J. Hoffman, *The Origins and Background of the Second World War* (New York, 1943), p. 270.

[7]C. E. Hughes, "The World Court," an address to the Bar Association of the city of New York, published in the *Congressional Record* (January 21, 1930), pp. 9–10.

[8]Dennison, op. cit., pp. 128–29.

[9]Hudson, *The World Court, 1921–38*, Document No. 18, pp. 292–97.

[10]Dennison, op. cit., p. 130.

[11]*Senate Report,* No. 758, 72nd Congress, 1st Session.

[12]New York *Times,* June 16 and 30, 1932.

[13]Ibid., January 7, 1934.

[14]Ibid., March 24, 1934.

[15]Clark M. Eichelberger, director of the League of Nations Association, said that his office had affidavits from people who had hastily signed this petition "against war," and afterward discovered that it was directed against the League and the Court. Ibid., May 18, 1934.

[16]Ibid., May 17, 1934.

Chapter VIII

[1]Denys Smith, *America and the Axis War* (New York, 1942), p. 97.

[2]*Congressional Record*, Vol. 79, Pt. 1, p. 468.

[3]Ibid., pp. 479–89. Naturally Johnson rejected any responsibility for the long delays about the Court. It was all Root's fault. "If Mr. Root had not at the instance of Sir Cecil Hurst manufactured something destroying our irreducible minimum of protection there would have been no delay." (P. 479.)

[4]New York *Times,* January 18, 1935.

[5]*Senate Executive Reports,* No. 1, 74th Congress, 1st Session.

[6]*Congressional Record,* Vol. 79, Pt. 1, p. 637; New York *Times,* January 19, 1935.

[7]Ibid., p. 965.

[8]Ibid., pp. 967–71.

[9]Ibid., pp. 1131, 1142.

[10]Ibid., p. 695.

[11]New York *Times,* January 21, 1935.

[12]Ibid., January 28, 1935.

[13]Seattle *Post-Intelligencer,* January 19, 1935.

[14]*Congressional Record* (February 4, 1935), Vol. 79, Pt. 1, pp. 1414, 1418.

[15]Stoner, op. cit., p. 260.

[16]New York *Times,* February 3, 1935.

[17]Ibid., January 31, 1935.

Chapter IX

[1]*Congressional Record,* April 13, 1938.

[2]Denys Smith, op. cit., pp. 203–05.

[3]Walter Lippmann, *United States Foreign Policy: Shield of the Republic* (Boston, 1943), p. 42.

[4]New York *Times*, October 4, 1939.

[5]Lippmann, op. cit., p. 37.

[6]Stoner, op. cit., p. 45. Stoner's book is a vivid account of an amazing personal crusade.

[7]Ibid., p. 162.

[8]Ibid., pp. 145, 156.

[9]Ibid., pp. 204–11.

[10]*In Re the World Court: The Judgment of the American Bar, 1921–34*, edited by Manley O. Hudson.

CHAPTER X

[1]Robert N. Wilkin, "America's Faith—A Call for Revival," New York *Times Magazine*, July 18, 1943.

[2]Kenneth Colegrove, *The American Senate and World Peace* (Vanguard Press, New York, 1944), pp. 202–9. The eleven laws upon which the twenty-six senators made their voting records were: Neutrality Revision; Selective Training and Service Bill; Limit Armed Forces to Western Hemisphere; Two-Billion Loan vs. Lend-Lease; Lend-Lease Bill; Transfer of Axis Ships; Extension of the Draft; Belligerent Zone Restrictions; Armed Ship Bill; Ship Seizure Bill; Second Lend-Lease Bill.

[3]Carl Hambro, *How to Win the Peace* (New York, 1942), p. 205.

[4]Princeton University Press, 1944, p. 36.

[5]June 28, 1944.

[6]This pamphlet may be obtained from the Superintendent of Documents or from Representative Bloom. See also the article in the New York *Times Magazine*, "A Summons against the Kiss of Death," by Senator Claude A. Pepper, December 12, 1943.

[7]Corwin, op. cit., p. 6.

[8]Wallace McClure, *International Executive Agreements* (New York, 1941). Especially pp. 252, 304, 367–87.

[9]See Colegrove, op. cit., p. 181.

[10]Quoted from Alexander Hamilton.

[11]From the introduction to *In Re the World Court: The Judgment of the American Bar, 1921–34*. Edited by Manley O. Hudson.

Index